Experiencing More with Less

An Intergenerational Curriculum for Camps, Retreats, and Other Educational Settings

Meredith Sommers Dregni

Foreword by Paul M. Longacre

HERALD PRESS
Scottdale, Pennsylvania
Kitchener, Ontario

EXPERIENCING MORE WITH LESS
Copyright © 1983 by Herald Press, Scottdale, Pa. 15683
    Published simultaneously in Canada by Herald Press,
    Kitchener, Ont. N2G 4M5
Library of Congress Catalog Card Number: 83-80954
International Standard Book Number: 0-8361-3334-X
Printed in the United States of America
Design by Tom Hershberger

83 84 85 86 87 88 10 9 8 7 6 5 4 3 2 1

Experiencing More with Less

*Dedicated to
the people of Nicaragua,
who are my teachers
and who
bring me hope.*

Contents

Foreword

Experiencing More with Less is an exciting "hands on" curriculum to help groups learn about responsible living. Its intergenerational approach strongly supports the teaching of values in such a way that they will "stick" beyond a session, a weekend, a week, or the duration of the study period.

Meredith Sommers Dregni creatively and faithfully captures and encapsulates the meaning of the five life standards of Doris Janzen Longacre's *Living More with Less* (Herald Press, 1980). Developed around one of these standards, each session in the curriculum incorporates biblical study and worship material. In addition, suggested songs, family activities, games, and exercises make a valuable contribution to the session.

Group leaders can follow the suggestions closely or use them as a point of departure for something unique to a given setting or need. The material is elastic, suitable to a wide variety of groups and occasions. At the same time, its purpose—helping individuals and families live more responsively—is clear and directed throughout.

What setting could be better than a camp or retreat center to explore such issues? The out-of-doors is an ideal place to learn to cherish the natural order. A retreat center is designed to encourage nurturing people. Dealing with the stewardship of resources and doing justice can be heavy agendas. *Experiencing More with Less* makes the subject of responsible living inviting and fun.

—Paul M. Longacre
Akron, Pennsylvania

Author's Preface

Managua, Nicaragua
November 11, 1982

I am sitting on a bench in Managua, watching the children play and the grownups converse. What I see around me are my teachers, the people of Nicaragua from whom I am learning. They are people who experience "living more with less" every day of their lives. Most Nicaraguans live on less than even the poorest North American. Yet, the people have milk, beans, and rice; they have clean drinking water. Literacy and health care for all are the country's priorities. What I am finding in Nicaragua is a country in which the first objective is to satisfy the basic needs of the population. The "more" of their lives is revealed to me in their strength, patience, and hope. The "more" can be seen in their spirit of caring for each other and for their land. I feel it in their ability to forgive those who persecute them. There is an excitement here of people creating their own future.

The country and its people are poor, but they are determined to use available resources efficiently and appropriately and also to create a society based on what they call the "logic of the poor." The people of Nicaragua are the embodiment of the resurrection of Jesus for me. Love and justice are inherent in their vision as they try to live out the teachings of Jesus and the example of the early church.

I am observing in Managua the five life standards spelled out by Doris Longacre in *Living More with Less:* Do Justice, Learn from the World Community, Nurture People, Cherish the Natural Order, and Nonconform Freely. This book, *Experiencing More with Less,* is designed to help people of North America experience the five life standards through song, worship, games, discussion, simulations, and celebration.

This experiential curriculum on lifestyle for families and "living units" has grown out of five years of experience by the staff of Hunger Action Coalition of Minnesota as educators and activists. As teachers, our staff know that the issues of hunger are understood when people make the connection between the root causes to the way in which they choose to live. "I know I must change" is an educated response of hunger seminar attendees. This is followed by "But how?" and then "Can I force changes on others who live with me because I can't do it alone."

The intention of *Experiencing More with Less* is to bring people together in small groups, like the "comunidades de base" of Nicaragua. Within these groups, new models for living can be shared and support for change can take place. By being together for an extended period of time, the experience will be remembered and understood.

This curriculum was developed for use at a United Church of Christ family camp in Minnesota in the summer of 1981. The United Methodist Church Board of Discipleship supported the writing of the original manuscript. A United Presbyterian family camp was the second test group.

And now it is offered to you, as a guide to be used creatively and adapted to your particular setting and group. I have enjoyed developing it. I hope you will share in that joy in your use of it.

—Meredith Sommers Dregni
Minneapolis, Minnesota

An Overview of This Curriculum

"I hear and I forget; I see and I remember; I do and I understand."—Chinese proverb

The premise underlying this curriculum is the belief that the actions and decisions of our daily lives flow from a set of religious affirmations and values. Often these values and beliefs have not been clarified or even recognized. They tend to reflect cultural trends rather than Christian faith. We can be led to awareness of the positive and negative impact of our value system on our own lives, on the lives of our global neighbors, and on the future of the planet. If offered more congruent alternatives and support for change, we will make changes. The purpose of *Experiencing More with Less* in an intergenerational setting is to provide the setting, models, and support where affirmations can be released and actions shared among family and friends.

The format for this curriculum is from the book *Living More with Less* by Doris Janzen Longacre. The book presents theoretical ideas on lifestyle analysis which lead to practical applications. Doris develops five life standards: Do Justice, Learn from the World Community, Nurture People, Cherish the Natural Order, and Nonconform Freely. Each day of the program uses one of the five standards. All standards are based in Scripture and provide topics for relating Bible study to everyday living.

Doris introduces the book by saying that it was written for those North Americans who know something is wrong with the way we live and want to do something about it. This leads to the questions of:

—Should the program committee promote the "more with less" theme, appealing to those families and individuals who are ready for change? Or,

—Should the theme be tucked into regular sessions and a more diverse group reached?

Both approaches are valid, but the leaders must be prepared to handle either situation.

The methods suggested are varied to take into account people of diverse ages and stages of awareness. There are times for:

Bible study	Games	Work projects
Lectures	Crafts	Hands-on experiences
Discussions	Singing	Worship
Simulations	Charades	Celebration
Values clarification	Audiovisuals	
Goal setting	Readings	

Purposes

1. To step back from the involvement and decisions of everyday life to gain a broader perspective on the connection and impact of a family or individual on the rest of the world.

2. To talk, play, and work together joyfully as a family unit, focusing on both shared and individual issues and values.

3. To have time simply to *be* with others, to discover that relationships with people have more value than relationships with things.

4. To have "hands-on" experiences with food, conservation, and the environment.

5. To discover creative alternatives for living.

Schedule

Schedule recommendations are for from 2 to 2½ hours per day, with additional ideas for special-interest sessions, games, audio-visuals, and the like.

Ages

This curriculum is designed for intergenerational groups. However, children under the age of five may need child care during some sessions. Children and adults may want some separate discussion time.

Setting and Time Framework

Camps or retreat centers are ideal settings for the curriculum, if there are facilities for work and play, study and worship. *It is important for people to be away from their familiar surroundings and to be together for an extended period of time.* There should be time enough to examine daily patterns and try out alternative ways of doing and being. The curriculum is designed for 5½ days.

This curriculum is also adaptable to other situations, such as a Lenten series of family evenings.

Leadership

Two leaders, plus volunteers. A leader-facilitator for the group sessions; a teacher or preacher who can coordinate vespers, introduce sessions, and chronicle the stories of the week. In an introductory letter to participants, ask for volunteers to help coordinate parts of the week, such as evening programs and morning worship. Ask teachers with skills such as cooking, building, or gardening to lead special-interest sessions. Tailor these sessions to the interests of your group.

In keeping with the standard of nurturing people, try to involve everyone in some way with responsibility for the program, the camp, and the well-being of others.

The book, *Living More with Less* (see resources), is the basic text for the leaders. The chapter order has been changed for the camp, with the more controversial sessions put toward the end of the week. Each day's curriculum includes an overview of the day, objectives for the day, and a plan with many suggestions, usually too many. Use what you wish and add your own. An asterisk indicates that the item (song, poem, or whatever) is included in this book.

Suggested Resource Material

(Other materials are referred to in specific sessions.)

Living More with Less, by Doris Janzen Longacre, Herald Press, 1980. The basic book for this curriculum.

Living More with Less, Study/Action Guide, by Delores Histand Friesen, Herald Press, 1981. A study guide written to highlight *Living More with Less.*

More-with-Less Cookbook, Doris Longacre's first book, a compilation of recipes from throughout the world, using nutrition and awareness of environment as underlying choices. Herald Press, 1978.

Lifestyle Change for Children, by Doris Shettel. Curriculum and activities for children, grades 1-6 (also suitable for adults). United Presbyterian Church, Office of Social Education, Room 1101, 475 Riverside Drive, New York, NY 10115.

A Covenant Group for Lifestyle Assessment, by William E. Gibson and Eco-Justice Task Force. Curriculum for adults (12 sessions, 2½ hours each). Available from UPC, same address as above.

Everflowing Streams. Songs for worship which use inclusive language and have a common vision of a world of peace and justice. Edited by Ruth C. Duck and Michael G. Bausch, Pilgrim Press, 1981.

The New Games Book, by Andrew Fluegelman, New Games Foundation, New York, Doubleday, 1976. Theory and description of "new games" which are active, noncompetitive, and fun.

Parenting for Peace and Justice, by Kathleen and James McGinnis, Orbis Books, 1981, $4.95. Program guide and handbook for parents and children.

How Do We Live in a Hungry World? 16 mm. film, 30 minutes, for high school age to adult. Shows several families trying to simplify their lifestyles. Discussion guide included. Available from United Methodist/film service, 1525 McGavock St., Nashville, TN 37203.

We're #1? Enough or Too Much, 16 mm, 27 min. High school age to adult. Deals with theology of enough. Steve Allen and John Schramm. Discussion guide included. Available from Lutheran Brotherhood Scheduling Center, 5000 Park Street N., St. Petersburg, FL 33709. No charge. Allow 4-6 weeks for delivery.

Remember Me, 16 mm., 27 min., youth-adult. A beautiful, sensitive film of children doing the "work of the world." Available from CROP, Elkhart, IN 46515.

INTRO SESSION

Living
More with
Less

Living More with Less

An Overview

To begin the session, ask the campers how they got to camp. If they drove, what made the vehicle go? What rules of the road did they have to follow? What signs and maps did they use? Compare their transportation to their life journey.

Fuel is needed to make the vehicle go. What fuel is needed for life? Certain rules of the road are needed so drivers know what they should do and what to expect from other drivers. Rules in life are necessary so people can live together and not hurt each other. The maps and signs guided them on their way to camp, as they do in life. Signs are like one's beliefs and values. They help guide our thinking and acting.

The values we will be using this week are called life standards. They come from a book, *Living More with Less,* written by Doris Janzen Longacre. These life standards will be our signposts as we try to be faithful to the life and teachings of Jesus.

This week we will talk about ways we would *like* to live. There are no absolute right ways or wrong ways. We want to discover ways in which we are more caring of other people, more gentle to our environment, and more loving of our God.

For the introductory session, becoming acquainted with other campers is the first objective. The second is becoming acquainted with the theme "Living More with Less" and the five life standards. Have copies of the book available.

After explaining the standards to the group, try a family or small-group charade game and apply the standards which fit. Do a charade on something the family does which is living more with less. If the charade is bicycle riding, for example, the family group acts it out with others trying to guess what they are doing. Then ask which life standards fit. For biking, most of them do.

The first day of camp is usually hectic, so plan accordingly. Short sessions without much lecturing are a good method. Singing familiar songs usually works well.

"It was said, 'Life is simple and it becomes complex.' And it is true. Then it was said, 'People are simple and they become complex.' But it is wrong, because knowing begins in the complexity of bewilderment and advances to the simplicity of comprehension."

Come, let us learn from the children and with the children. Let us be like them.

PLAN FOR THE DAY

Biblical Reference

Luke 12:22-31. The flowers never have to spin or weave.

Objectives of the Day

1. To learn to know each other.
2. To become acquainted with the theme "Living More with Less" and the five life standards.

Time	Activities and Comments	Equipment and Supplies
20 min.	*Making name tags.* Be creative and conserving. For example, try using scraps of lumber with holes for yarn to hang around neck, with name written with marker.	lumber, marker, yarn
20 min.	*Get-acquainted game.* Make a list of characteristics which participants may have. Have them find out who has them by asking questions. As an example, name someone who: —has lived on a farm. —plays a guitar. —walks to school. —doesn't have a TV video game.	paper and pencils
15 min.	*Overview of the theme* of the sessions, schedules, and activities.	
15 min.	*Presentation of the five life standards.* See the first five chapters of *Living More with Less.* Use your own words and plenty of examples. Hand out copies (from pages 19 and 20).	*Living More with Less* Doris Janzen Longacre Herald Press, 1980
40 min. or so	*Family charades.* Allow about five minutes for family or small	Handout with life standards*

groups to discuss something
they do which is living more
with less. Have them act out the
charade for the whole group to
try to guess what it is. Apply the
life standards which may fit.

"Shaker Welcome" (see below).

Vespers and singing around
the campfire.

Shaker Welcome Song

Welcome here, welcome here!
All be alive and of good cheer!
We have the bread all baked
    complete
And we have the drink, it's very
    sweet.

Welcome here, welcome here!
All be alive and of good cheer!
Grace and peace be unto you
From God most high, the Lord
    of truth.

FIVE LIFE STANDARDS

"Living more with less" means that by using less of the world's resources we can actually gain more for ourselves and for others. It means living more joyfully, freely, and creatively. Living more with less isn't necessarily simple living. It may be more complex as we realize that even small decisions have huge effects on our environment and global neighbors. Our goal is to make responsible choices.

Life standards are principles developed by Doris Longacre which helped her to make decisions. Life standards describe a way of life characterized by timeless values and commitments. Rather than "lifestyle" which connotes a more temporary style of living, life standards are a way of life governed by permanent and firm principles of living. The suggested standards are:

1. Learn from the World Community

Global interdependence is a fact. The way we live affects the world community and vice versa. Other nations can help us with our problems of over-, under-, and mal-development. For example, we can learn about effects of the atom bomb from Japan; school lunch programs from China; living without disposables from almost every country; valuing family and friendship above money from Africa. To do this, we have to be open to hear what others have to say and to observe how others live. Second, we must replace the attitude which says, "We're number 1," with, "We're all citizens of the world."

2. Cherish the Natural Order

The earth is a common possession of all humanity, today and for generations to come. We have a responsibility to fit the way we live into the environment, rather than to reshape the environment to our whims. For example, we need not give up manufacturing, but we must make ethical decisions about factory pollution and human health.

3. Nurture People

In the hard decisions of living, to choose that which nurtures people is sometimes the most difficult. The standard of the nurturer is care, not efficiency. The nurturer serves the land, the household, the community, and others; thinks in terms of character, conditions, quality, and kind; is committed to reduce stress and foster health; is concerned with providing security through loving relations, not through material possessions or power structures.

4. Do Justice

Every decision we make has a ripple effect both on those in our daily lives and those around the world. Every time we pump gas into a car, for example, we are part of the economic and political sphere. Doing justice occurs when we think through the effects of our actions and make a choice which benefits, or at least is less harmful to, others. Our influence may be small, but the composite influence of many is enormous. It is important to exercise our responsibilities as public policy advocates for justice to make sure that our life standards are directly felt.

5. Nonconform Freely

To live more with less is to oppose the "bigger and better" slogans of our society. To nonconform freely we must truly believe in the freedom of not being convinced by advertising and enslaved to material things. Instead of asking, "Can we afford what we want?" a new question emerges, "Do we need what we can afford?"

> If you head into unfamiliar woods, you had better find companions first.
> If you want to buck traffic, organize a convoy.
> To nonconform freely, we must strengthen each other.
> —from *Living More with Less*

SESSION 1

Learn from the World Community

Learn from the World Community

An Overview

God created all races and made them live over the whole earth, according to Acts 17:26. God in wisdom, created differences, as well as similarities. We can become frightened and closed off from other people because of these differences, or our lives can be enriched and challenged by them.

Have you heard the comment, "Those poor people in other countries don't value life like we do? They are used to being hungry, being without work, having their babies die." The purpose of this session is to allow people to experience the universal feelings of love, hope, and despair.

The morning worship or session can begin with a journey inward, to the time when we were all refugees, coming to this country, seeking a better, safer life.

Then share the simulation of *Family Life in Guatemala*, designed to provide the experience of identifying with a specific person in Guatemala and the choices which that person must make. This is adapted from an actual case study made in 1980.

An excellent film to use during the day is *Remember Me*. It shows children in the Third World who, because of economic conditions, must spend their childhoods in work. The film is beautifully and sensitively made.

The theme "Learn from the World Community" has many possibilities for food, games, songs, costumes, and crafts, some of which are included. If possible, ask the cooks to prepare a foreign meal, such as Egyptian Kusherie or Vietnam Fried Rice (recipes in the *More-with-Less Cookbook*, also by Doris Longacre). For a special-interest session, prepare tofu (soybean curd), available in most food cooperatives or health food stores.

Use your imagination for an evening celebration and vesper. You could include songs, crafts, and stories from the day in a puppet show. Description and instructions for an African Harvest Festival and Vietnamese New Year appear in *Lifestyle Change for Children* by Doris Shettel, pages 23-26.

PLAN FOR THE DAY

Biblical Reference

Acts 17:24-28. We are all God's children.

Objectives of the Day

1. To sensitize participants to other people in the world, especially the poor.

2. To gain appreciation for differences and similarities in all people.

Time	Activities and Comments	Equipment and Supplies
15 min.	*Morning worship.* Acts 17:24-28. You can include *Reliving the Past*, a meditation and fantasy.	The Bible *Reliving the Past**
	Songs: "Children's March" "Planting Rice"	Songs*
25 min.	*Film,* "Remember Me," stories of children of the Third World and discussion.	*Remember Me,* free from CWS/CROP P.O. Box 968 Elkhart, IN 46515 Screen 16 mm. projector
40 min.	*A simulation,* "Family Life in Guatemala." Participants become members of a Guatemalan family, planning a week's budget and activities.	World Map Leader's Guide*
	Poem, "Poverty Is Relative" by Judith Mattison.	Poem*
	Special-interest session. Food from Other Lands. Try a cooking session using tofu (soybean	*The Book of Tofu* Autumn Press 1318 Beacon St.

curd) or tempura, two of the most nutritious protein sources and widely used foods. Or bake bread from other countries—tortillas, pita bread, or Irish soda bread.

International games. Soccer is one of the most popular. Switch players from team to team with every score for a less competitive game.

Blind Man's Bluff, a Chippewa game, is a children's favorite. Blindfold one person. Have everyone scatter within limits and the blindfolded person try to identity the others.

Craft. Try paper bag or finger puppets, popular in Great Britain. Dramatize a story, such as "The Ugly Duckling" by Hans Christian Andersen

Or make clay pots using a coil of clay wrapped and circled until a pot is formed. This is basic to most countries.

Evening celebration;
Israeli Circle Dance
or
African Harvest Festival
or
Vietnam New Year.
(See description in book listed at the right.)

If any of the participants have their own traditions, ask them to teach the customs to the group.

Brookline, MA
02146
or
Diet for a Small Planet
F. M. Lappé
Ballantine Books, New York

Lifestyle Change for Children
Doris Shettel
475 Riverside Drive
Room 1101
New York, NY
10115

RELIVING THE PAST

A quiet exercise for an intergenerational group.

Purpose

To relive in our minds the lives and feelings of our ancestors coming to a new land as immigrants to make us sensitive to our global neighbors and refugees.

Setting

A quiet place where people can be comfortable and hear the leader.

Time

About 10 minutes.

Instructions

1. Have participants close their eyes and relax their bodies and minds.

2. Read the following narrative slowly or tell it in your own words. Pause to let pictures come into people's minds.

"If you are not a Native American, you or your ancestors emigrated from another country.... At some time, your forebears made, or had made for them, the decision to emigrate, to leave their ancestral home and familiar culture.... They were refugees....

It was probably hard to depart ... leaving the land and water and trees they had always known ... to leave the house, the kitchen, the bedroom where they lived ... brothers, sisters, parents, children, friends....

Imagine their feelings.... Were they scared, hopeful, sad?

They probably were all three.... They had hope, coming to this new land, hope for safety, better jobs, and better lives for their children.

Perhaps they arrived by boat and passed the Statue of Liberty, where these words are written for all who come:

> Give me your tired, your poor,
> Your huddled masses yearning to breathe free,
> The wretched refuse of your teeming shore.
> Send these, the homeless, tempest-tossed to me,
> I lift my lamp beside the golden door!

People are still coming. They come for many of the same reasons ... safety, jobs, a better life for their children. They have the same feelings of fear ... of hope ... of sadness.

Reflect on someone who came to this country recently. What are you learning from him or her about the world community?

3. Bring the group into the present. Have someone read this poem as a closing.

WELCOMING REFUGEES
By Judith Mattison

For decades immigrants came
to our welcoming shores.
They worked
    learned
      developed this land.
Refugees
bringing desire and strength.
We are diverse and strong
because they came.

Now that we have so much,
let us look back
in gratitude
and welcome more immigrants.
New people
offering greater diversity
and additional strengths.
We do not choose
to keep only for ourselves.
We choose to share
because we have much
and it is right
to give refugees
a home.

—From *Help Me Adapt, Lord,* used by permission.

FAMILY LIFE IN GUATEMALA

A simulation experience of the economic, political, and social stress on family structures in a Guatemalan village, taken from a case study.

Objective

To provide North Americans with the experience of a typical village family in a Third World setting, thus developing a personal identity with the difficulties and joys of life among a poor community.

Ages

About eight years and up.

Group Size

At least six, up to 100, divided into small groups (families).

Time

20 minutes for exercise, 20 minutes for discussion, minimum.

Materials

Piece of paper and pencil for each group. Map to show where Guatemala is.

Preparation

Copy expenditures chart on newsprint for all to see.

Expenditures		Recommended (Not Required) Dietary Allowances*
Corn (for tortillas)	10¢ pound	7 pounds
Dried beans	30¢ pound	3½ pounds
Rice	20¢ pound	3½ pounds
Chicken	75¢ pound	3 pounds, or an extra 2 lbs. beans
Eggs	10¢ egg	7
Milk	10¢ cup	21 cups
Soda pop	20¢ bottle	
Beer	50¢ bottle	
Candles	10¢ week	
Firewood for cooking	$2.50 week	
Visit to doctor	$1.00	
Medicine	50¢ to $5.00	
Offering to church	at least 5¢	*for the family per week

Background Information. Give these facts to the group before the exercise, either by reading, as a handout or on newsprint.

- Guatemala is known for its extraordinary beauty, its pre-Columbian ruins, its rich farmland, and the dignity of its people.
- Guatemala has 7¼ million inhabitants in a country the size of Tennessee. About 65 percent of the people are Indian who speak Mayan; the other 35 percent are Spanish-speaking *mestizos*.
- Half of the population has an annual average per capita income of about $75.

- Four out of five of the children under five years suffer from malnutrition; one out of five dies before four years old.
- About 2 percent of the farms control 72 percent of the productive land and use it to produce coffee, sugar, cotton, beef, bananas, and natural rubber, primarily for export.
- Thirty percent of the exports go to the United States.
- There is 1 teacher for every 400 children of school age. There is 1 soldier for every 140 citizens.
- In a recent year, the U.S. Department of Commerce approved a $3.2 million license for the commercial cash sale to Guatemala of 150 military trucks and jeeps.
- Many North American corporations do business in Guatemala, such as Coca-Cola, Pillsbury, Cargill, Weyerhauser, Federal Cartridge Corporation of Minneapolis, Del Monte, Goodyear Rubber, Philip Morris, Bank of America.

Situation

Divide the group into "families" of about six or seven persons. Have the members take on the following roles:

Mario Tzul, the father. You inherited your one acre of land from your father. You have tried to live on the crops the land produces but there is only half of what your family needs just to survive. Consequently, you sell the crops to buy corn and rice. You also work six days a week at the nearby coffee plantation, 10-12 hours a day. For all of this, you earn $15 per week, but work is seasonal and lasts about eight months a year. (In 1980, the workers' strike raised minimum wage to $3.20 a day, but this is rarely paid.)

Carman Tzul, the mother. You do the cooking and you try to keep your one-room home, the clothes and the children clean, but the only water source is a well one mile away. You make the trek daily with Juanita, carrying the water in a pot on your head. You take in laundry from the coffee plantation owner's family. For this, you earn $2.50 a week.

Juanita Tzul, 12-year-old daughter. You used to go to school but now you are needed at home to help with the laundry your mother takes in.

Carlos Tzul, 10-year-old son. You go to the village school, an hour's walk from home. You gather firewood to sell after school to buy books for school and for an occasional soda pop.

Jose Tzul, 8-year-old son. You suffered malnutrition as a child. From lack of vitamin A, your eyesight is poor and you are very small. You do not go to school.

Baby Maria, 6 months. You are greatly treasured by your family, as two children died before you were born.

Grandmother Tzul. Although you are only 46 years old, you look and feel very old. You used to weave and sew most of the family's clothing, but thread costs too much now and it is cheaper to buy cloth made in Taiwan and El Salvador. You help with child care and you tell stories of your ancestors to the children.

Exercise

Your task as a family is to plan your family budget and activities for the next week. After about five minutes, the leader should visit the families to offer one or more of the options, one at a time. Keep the exercise moving and encourage creative, yet caring, responses.

OPTIONS

Carlos may work on the coffee plantation instead of going to school. Wage: $5.00 per week.

Juanita may go to live with a wealthy family in town and care for their children. Wage: food, housing, $1.00 per month.

Grandmother becomes ill. A visit to the doctor is recommended but the doctor is five miles away. Medicine, if bought, will cost $1.50.

Other children could gather firewood for the family to save $2.50.

Baby Maria is sick. Carman has heard an advertisement on the radio that infant formula helps babies become healthier. Cost: 25¢/day. If Carman quits breast feeding, she cannot begin again.

A loan is available from the coffee plantation store. Interest rate is 10 percent per month.

Workers on the coffee plantation organize a labor union and decide to go on strike. Unions are officially guaranteed by the constitution but only 2 percent of the work force is unionized. The workers are asking for a raise of $5.00 per week, but the plantation has threatened to bring in a death squad. If Mario joins the union he may lose his job or his life; if he doesn't join, he will be ostracized by other workers and his life could be in danger.

Ending

As the exercise progresses, the family members may feel the frustration of their roles and their life/death conflict in making decisions. Help the group see this is a family who cares about one another. Call the exercise to a close before the group is too discouraged.

For final discussion, ask participants how they felt during the exercise and about their decisions, as they report on their experience. Discuss: How are our lifestyles in North America affected by the way the Tzuls live? How are the Tzuls affected by our lives?

—Information from Minnesota Guatemala Solidarity Committee, NACLA publications, *Central America Report* and *Multinational Monitor.*

POVERTY IS RELATIVE
By Judith Mattison

When I feel poor
I open a book
and look at pictures
of the rest of the world—
the children of Calcutta,
the women of Ethiopia,
the men of Mexico.
Poverty is relative,
and I am not one of the world's poor.
If I spend my time
thinking about the upper crust
and envying them,
I forget that a crust of bread
would sustain a person
a few hours longer
if I would share it.
As near as Detroit
and Appalachia
is the rope of poverty
which strangles hope and
determination.
Look again at the pictures.
I am not poor.

—From *Help Me Adapt, Lord,* used by permission

Planting Rice

Filipino Folk Song

1. {Plant-ing rice is nev-er fun, Bent from morn 'til set of sun.
   Oh, my back is like to break, Oh, my bones with damp-ness ache,

2. {When the ear-ly sun-beams break, You will won-der as you wake,
   It is hard to be so poor, And such sor-ry pain en-dure,

Can-not stand and can-not sit, Can-not rest a lit-tle bit.
And my legs are numb and set From their soak-ing in the wet.

2. In what mud-dy neigh-bor-hood There is work and pleas-ant food.

{Plant-ing rice is no fun. Bent from morn 'til set of sun.
Oh, my back! Like to break, Oh, my bones with damp-ness ache.

Can-not stand, can-not sit, Can-not rest a lit-tle bit!
And my legs are numb and set From their soak-ing in the wet.

You must move your arms a-bout, Or you'll find you'll be with-out!

From *Hi! Neighbor.* 1957. U.S. Committee for UNICEF.

Children's March

Clyde Thompson

We are all God's chil-dren— and we all can live

1. Wheth-er big, wheth-er small, wheth-er short, wheth-er tall, wheth-er
2. Ev-er young, ev-er old, ev-er fear-ful, ev-er bold, ev-er
3. For the spir-it with-in— will nev-er, nev-er die and the

weak, wheth-er strong, wheth-er right or wheth-er wrong, You are
meek, ev-er brave, ev-er need-ing to be saved, Ev-er
feel-ing with-in— will al-ways make us try. We are

fine, you are his, You are life go-ing on— and
hum-ble, ev-er proud, ev-er need-ing to be found— we
his; we are one with the Spir-it and the Son— we

on —
are ——— we are
are ——— we are ——— we are ———

Reprinted by permission.

SESSION 2

Cherish the Natural Order

Cherish the Natural Order

An Overview

The value which a society places upon the land, air, and water can be easily observed by looking at the condition of their environment. Is the environment abused by overcultivation of the land, pollution of the air and water, and trash on the ground? Or is the environment cared for and respected, with future generations in mind? A Native American adage goes, "Decisions today are made with regard for the next seven generations."

"Can our Judeo-Christian creation story be compatible with the needs of the earth?" asks Elizabeth Dodson Gray in her book *Green Paradise Lost.* She writes that we must redefine the emphasis of the hierarchy in which "man" is given higher rank and dominance over the lower-ranked plants and animals. This hierarchy is destructive when humans try to outdo God with decisions about the earth and plants and animals. In place of dominion, E. D. Gray suggests we must emphasize that God's covenant of creation is with *all* creation, and puts value on all parts of nature. No part is judged to be better than or less than any other part. There is purpose in all creation, even if humans can't understand it. Uniqueness and interrelatedness of all creation must be stressed.

For the session on "Cherish the Natural Order" it is important to clarify basic attitudes and values about the environment, because this determines subsequent actions. The session, therefore, begins with a Bible study on creation and stewardship in which children and adults can participate.

Interrelatedness and interconnectedness are like a circle with other circles interlinked. People, fish, earthworms, dirt, water, air, eagles, mosquitoes ... all are interdependent. If harm comes to one of these, all parts of creation are affected. A "new game" which demonstrates interconnectedness is recommended. Take a few minutes after the game to talk about connections.

There are two suggested films: "1000 Suns" emphasizes in an artistic form the responsible use of energy. "Toast" documents the journey of wheat to bread to burned toast and the energy consumed on the trip.

Brownout, Blackout is an exercise for individuals or family groups on energy use in the home. Participants are asked to write down all the things they use which require electricity. Then there is a brownout, then a blackout. This exercise forces participants to look at their dependence on centralized electrical power and lack of alternatives.

An excellent book for parents and teachers to use with children on environmental attitudes and awareness is *Sharing Nature with Children,* by Joseph Cornell, Ananda Publications, 14618 Tyler Foote Rd., Nevada City, CA 95959.

A nature hike, focusing on interconnectedness, can be an outdoors learning experience. For an action project, set up recycling centers around the camp. Explain how recycling saves resources. If there are solar or wind generators, use these as demonstrations of appropriate technology.

Try a special interest session on "wild" foods, if you have a knowledgeable person to lead it. Or follow the enclosed session plan on "Some seeds we plant and some seeds we eat."

For vespers, suggest a Native American theme of "Spirit of the Earth." Try a quiet meditation, listening to the sounds of the night.

PLAN FOR THE DAY

Biblical Reference

Psalms 24:1 and 104:24. The earth is the Lord's and the fulness thereof.

Objectives of the Day

1. To understand that we are caretakers of God's gifts.
2. To analyze our energy use.
3. To take an action or learn a new skill.

Time	Activities and Comments	Equipment and Supplies
15 min.	*Morning worship.* Pair adult and child to read Psalms 24:1 and 104:24. Have them talk about what those verses say to them about God and creation. Share a short sermon on relating our values toward our environment and the future. "Parapets of the Future" by E. D. Gray is included as a background piece.	Bibles "Parapets of the Future"*

	Songs:	
	"For the Beauty of the Earth"	Hymnbooks
	"Blue Is the Sky"	Song*
10-15 min.	*Interconnectedness*, a new game with symbolism	Game*
12-15 min.	*Films* (either is appropriate): "1000 Suns," Bullfrog Films, Oley, PA 19547. "Toast," Earth Chronicles. May be available from energy library or school library.	16 mm. projector Screen
20 min.	*Brownout, Blackout*, an exercise on energy use in the home. In family units or small groups, have members write down as many things as they can think of which use electricity in their home. Then pose this situation: "There is too much demand for electricity today, so there is a brownout for the rest of the day. This actually happened recently in New York and electricity was cut by 50 percent." Have the groups decide what adjustments they would make at home to cut their electrical use in half. Then go to a blackout, no electricity for the rest of the week.	Paper Pencils Newsprint Markers, tape Charts*

How will they manage? What is hardest to do without? Are there alternative energy sources?

Now, give the groups newsprint and marker to write down or draw pictures of ways their family can use less energy. Tape up when finished.

For variety, do the same exercise with appliances which use gas, oil, batteries.

Hand out *Tips for Energy Savers*, available free from U.S. Department of Energy, Pueblo, CO 81009.   *Energy Savers' Tips*

45 min.   *Nature hike.* To discover relationship of earth, water, air, animals, plants.
The hike can be in the form of a scavenger hunt, but for observation, not collection of items. List things the groups could find and have them check them off, perhaps on a map of the area.
Or have a litter hunt. Place a litter box in a central location and measure the amount gathered.

45 min.   *Make a recycling station.*
Explain the reasons for recycling paper, tin, aluminum, plastic, and glass. Trace these products to their origin—for example, tin from Bolivia, aluminum from Jamaica.
Using boxes, label the objects to be recycled. Place near kitchen, craft room, or office—wherever there are recyclable materials.

Poem, "Recycling Is Natural" by   Poem*
Judith Mattison

Craft (using materials from nature).
Try weaving long grasses, sticks, leaves.
Dye eggs or fabrics with onion skins.
Make mobiles of driftwood.

Special interest session: Using the sun to heat and cool. As a simple project, make a solar-cooler by placing wet towels over a box placed in the sunlight. The evaporation of the water cools the interior of the box. Place foods in box to stay cool. Keep towels wet. For a more difficult project, build a window-box solar collector. Plans are available in *New Shelter* magazine. Or take a black, 50 gallon drum, fill with water, set in sun raised above the ground. When the water is warm, use it for washing.

Special interest session on wild foods. With a knowledgeable person or picture book, identify, collect, prepare, and eat wild foods such as cattails, berries, red sumac berries, dandelion greens

Or do a session on "Some seeds we plant and some seeds we eat."

Plan*

Vespers. Try a Native American theme on the "Spirit of the Earth." For readings, see *Touch the Earth* by T. C. McLuhan, Simon & Shuster, New York, 1971.

PARAPETS OF THE FUTURE
By Elizabeth Dodson Gray

"Watchman! Tell us of the night, what its signs of promise are!"

Futurists are watchmen perched in their towers of forecasting, forethinking, trend extrapolations, and alternative scenarios for the future. Futurists gaze out into the mists of time ahead, looking for signs of promise or disaster. Some 6,000 futurists from more than 40 countries gathered in Toronto some time ago for the First Global Conference on the Future. They shared binoculars, crystal balls, and computer printouts about the things ahead on our time-horizons.

What was most extraordinary about this First Global Conference on the Future was that Old Testament prophets Isaiah and Jeremiah would have seemed quite at home with the basic themes.

The conference opened with a star-studded series of three plenary panels in which futurists such as Lester Brown, Hazel Henderson, Aurelio Peccei, Bertrand de Jouvenal, Magda McHale, Robert Theobald, and Maurice Strong spoke briefly. Almost all agreed that the coalescing problems of population, food, water, energy, and environment hover over us like threatening storm clouds. Judgment, like the hosts of the Assyrian army, can be seen on the horizon.

These grim portents are spelled out and given greater emphasis by *The Global 2000 Report to the President,* which was released in Washington, D.C., on the last day of the conference. U.S. farmlands growing corn, for example, are losing topsoil at an average rate of 20 tons per acre per year. Tropical rainforests are being cut at the rate of an area half the size of California each year. By the year 2000, forty percent of the remaining tropical forests will have been destroyed. In *The Sinking Ark,* environmental scientist Norman Myers estimates we are losing one plant or animal species daily. By the mid-to-late 1980s we will be losing one species an hour because we are destroying entire habitats. By 2000 the rate of loss of species will be one hundred species a day.

The message is clear. Human society cannot go on as it has been and is now—manufacturing without recycling; strewing toxic wastes upon soil, waters, and the air; rapidly depleting remaining fossil fuels; covering with cement and asphalt some of the best agricultural soils; pursuing agricultural practices that permit precious and irreplaceable topsoil to blow or wash away. In our rush to have material growth and material progress, we have been oblivious to the constraints inherent in biological systems and a finite earth.

Mrs. Gray works with the Bolton Institute for a Sustainable Future, Wellesley, Massachusetts. The article is reprinted by permission.

But how to change?

The first clarion call of warning was the controversial Club of Rome Report *The Limits to Growth* (1972). *Limits* concluded with an expressed hope that "value change" would allow society to change its behavior. The question was: Would such a value change take place?

A startling feature of the Toronto conference was the oft-expressed idea that the hoped-for value change is indeed taking place. William Harman, associate director of the prestigious Stanford Research Institute (SRI), reporting in his keynote address on research done at SRI, indicated that we are now in the midst of such a transformation and that it is of the magnitude of the Renaissance or Protestant Reformation. Harman expressed his conviction that there is to be found at the core of this great transformation of values the essence of truth that is to be found in all the world's great religions.

Isaiah and Jeremiah would have been pleased. A call to repentance, and a role for religion in the conversion process! Harman was not alone in sounding this theme. Several of the 21 concurrent "tracks" of the many-faceted conference dealt with what was variously called "transition," "transformation," "consciousness change," "value change," and "a paradigm shift."

At another panel about "Re-envisioning Reality" individual panelists spoke about their own sense of "inner transformation," a "journey" into a new sense of selfhood that had a spiritual dimension. They had in this process discovered new communities with others whose lives have been undergoing similar changes.

The Canadian financier and industrialist Maurice Strong had been asked to sum up the conference. Strong had been the first head of the UN Environment Program. "We must accommodate the spiritual needs of people in major institutions," he said, noting that he was surprised at this theme sounding through the conference. He said in his judgment the best epochs in human history occurred at times when business and economics were secondary to intellectual, cultural, and spiritual values—not when business was dominant in the culture. Ours has been such a period of business dominance, he said, but that is beginning to change.

"We are now seeing a convergence of physical, social, and moral movements," Strong said. "Morals and values used to be seen as froth. We are now realizing that Sharing and Caring are not pious ideals but sound principles for living upon and caring for this planet."

The Old Testament prophet Amos never used words such as "sharing" and "caring." But those words are similar in import to Amos's call to a pervasive justice in society. Let us be sure we hear the message, even though it comes now in different words.

INTERCONNECTEDNESS
A new game with symbolism.

The purpose of interconnectedness is for a mass of people to remain connected but to become untangled.

Form circles of from 10-12 players, standing close together. Everyone place both hands in the center and find two other hands to hold, but not those next to you or both belonging to the same body. Now, try to untangle. Hands can twist around but should not separate. Bodies can climb or lie down.

When the mass becomes untangled, usually into one large or two interconnected circles, stop and look for symbolism in the game which pertains to our environment or to changing lifestyles.

—Adapted from *The New Games Book*

RECYCLING IS NATURAL
By Judith Mattison

The order of creation is remarkable.
Nothing disappears completely.
Fire and wood
turn to heat
      smoke
      carbon.
Leaves become humus for future growth.

The order of people
leaves much to be desired.
We do not honor the earth,
leaves to humus to trees.
We drop our litter,
      our aluminum
      our glass and plastic
and hope it will disappear.

God watches our folly
and waits for us to realize
his world needs protection
and responsible care.
Recycling is consistent
with God's plan.
Am I part of the order of creation?

—From *Help Me Adapt, Lord,* used by permission.

Blue Is the Sky

G. D. N.
Refrain   Gunnar D. Nielson

Blue   is   the   sky,   and   gen - tle   winds   are   blow - ing,

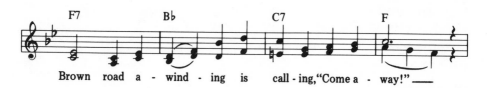

Brown   road a - wind - ing   is   call - ing, "Come a - way!" __

Where   flow - ers   bloom   and   qui - et   streams   are   flow - ing,

There   let   us   roam   this   bless - ed   live - long __ day!

1. Join   our   com - pa - ny   of   hik - ing - lik - ing   na - ture - seek - ers,
2. Take   your   leave   from   books,   our   trus - ty, dus - ty friends and   ty - rants,

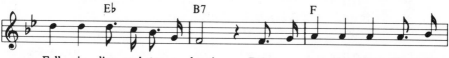

Fall   in   line   and   step a - long!   Drive a - way   the   blues, Sing the
And   de - clare your lib - er - ty!   Join   our   hap - py   song   As   we

song   you   choose, You   will   find   your   sec - ond   wind   in   song.
stride a - long   For   to - day   we   will   be   gay   and   free.

Danish Hiking Song Tr. by Knudson, © 1941, D.A.Y.P.L.; Alt. ADZ, 1962, CRS, Inc.
Used by permission of Grand View College, Des Moines, Iowa.

SOME SEEDS WE PLANT AND SOME SEEDS WE EAT

Objective

The children will discover the seeds that are good to eat.

Materials

Sunflower seeds
Pumpkin seeds
Caraway seeds
Poppy seeds
Sesame seeds
Anise seeds

Procedure

1. Are seeds useful to us?

   Seeds are very special. Life comes from seeds. Seeds are very good food for us because they are rich in vitamins and minerals.
2. What can you do with seeds?

   Seeds may be planted, sprouted, put on bread, put in salads and eaten for snacks.
3. Which seeds have you eaten?

   In what foods do you like seeds? What kind of seeds are good for in-between meal snacks?
4. Have the children taste pumpkin and sunflower seeds.

   Discuss taste, softness, hardness, size, and color. Have the children draw pumpkins and sunflowers. Make the sunflowers huge and hang them on the wall.
5. Visit a farm and get a pumpkin. Make a jack-o-lantern.

   Roast the seeds. Sprinkle lightly with salt. They are delicious sprinkled on salad.
6. Roast sesame seeds in the oven on a cookie sheet. Crush sesame seeds with a mortar and pestle. Sprinkle lightly with salt. They are delicious when sprinkled on a salad.

—Reprinted by permission from *Creative Food Experiences for Children*, available from Center for Science in the Public Interest, 1755 S St., N.W., Washington, DC 20009, copyright 1980.

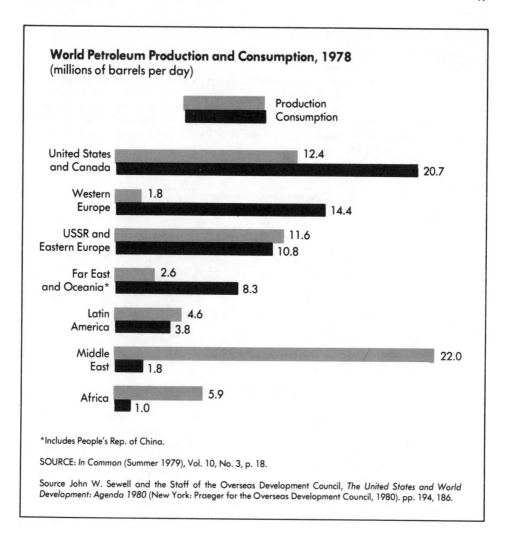

World Petroleum Production and Consumption, 1978
(millions of barrels per day)

Production
Consumption

United States and Canada	12.4 / 20.7
Western Europe	1.8 / 14.4
USSR and Eastern Europe	11.6 / 10.8
Far East and Oceania*	2.6 / 8.3
Latin America	4.6 / 3.8
Middle East	22.0 / 1.8
Africa	5.9 / 1.0

*Includes People's Rep. of China.

SOURCE: *In Common* (Summer 1979), Vol. 10, No. 3, p. 18.

Source John W. Sewell and the Staff of the Overseas Development Council, *The United States and World Development: Agenda 1980* (New York: Praeger for the Overseas Development Council, 1980). pp. 194, 186.

Per Capita Energy Consumption for Various Countries
(kilograms of coal equivalent, 1978)

Country	kg	Country	kg
United States	11,374	China	805
Canada	9,930	Philippines	339
West Germany	6,015	Thailand	327
USSR	5,500	India	176
United Kingdom	5,212	Pakistan	172
Japan	3,825	Indonesia	278
Mexico	1,384	Nigeria	106
Brazil	731	Bangladesh	43

Source: The World Bank, *World Development Report, 1980* (New York: Oxford University Press for the World Bank, 1980) pp. 122, 123.

Composition of Exports, 1960 and 1977
($ millions and percentages)

Between 1960 and 1977, reliance on primary products for export earnings decreased for developed market economies, centrally planned economies, and even developing market economies. However, while the developed market economies and centrally planned economies rely on primary products for 22.2 per cent and 38.6 per cent of their export earnings, respectively, the developing market economies still rely on primary products for some 80.6 per cent of their export earnings.

Developed Market Economies

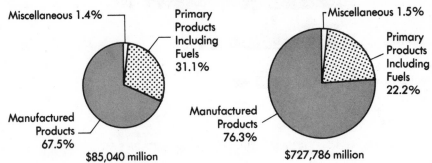

Developing Market Economies

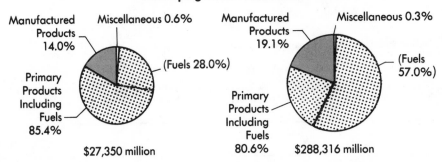

Centrally Planned Economies

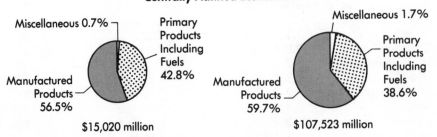

[1]World trade totaled $127,410 million in 1960 and $1,123,624 million in 1977.

SOURCES: ODC table based on U.N., *Monthly Bulletin*, Vol. 19, No. 3, March 1965, Special Table E, and Vol. 33, No. 5, May 1979, Special Table D.

Estimated Energy Data

Product	Representative Operating Wattage	No. of Uses Per Year	Time/Use (Min.)	Hours/ Year	% Actual "On" Time*	kWh/** Year
Blanket	150	180	480.0	1440.0	50	108.0
Blender	300	293	0.5	2.4	100	0.7
Can Opener	100	1000	0.2	3.3	100	0.3
Coffee Percolator—Brew	600	600	15.0	150.0	100	90.0
—Warm Cycle	80	600	60.0	600.0	100	48.0
Drip Coffee Maker—Brew	1100	600	9.5	95.0	100	104.5
—Warm Cycle	70	600	60.0	600.0	100	42.0
Corn Popper—Hot Air	1400	100	5.0	8.3	100 ·	11.6
—Oil	575	100	9.0	15.0	100	8.6
Curling Iron	40	300	10.0	50.0	82	1.6
Deep Fryer	1500	50	50.0	41.6	50	31.2
Food Processor	370	130	1.0	2.5	100	0.9
Fry Pan	1200	180	45.0	135.0	62	100.4
Hairdryer—Hand-Held	1000	250	8.0	33.3	100	33.3
Ice-Cream Freezer	130	6	45.0	4.5	100	0.6
Iron	1100	52	120.0	104.0	52	59.5
Kettle	1500	600	5.0	50.0	100	75.0
Knife	95	90	5.0	7.5	100	0.7
Lighted Mirror						
—Incandescent	50	650	10.0	108.3	100	5.4
—Fluorescent	20	650	10.0	108.3	100	2.2
Mixer—Hand	100	150	5.0	12.5	100	1.3
—Stand	150	75	8.0	10.0	100	1.5
Roaster	1425	12	360.0	72.0	58	60.0
Shaver	15	365	5.0	30.0	100	0.5
Slow Cooker	200	104	400.0	693.0	100	138.6
Toaster	1100	700	3.0	35.0	100	38.5
Toaster/Oven—Toasting	1500	500	3.0	25.0	100	37.5
—Oven	1500	280	30.0	140.0	26	54.6
Waffle/Sandwich Grill	1200	52	30.0	26.0	80	24.9
Yogurt Maker	25	26	600.0	260.0	40	2.6

*Factor for the effect of on-off cycling in thermostatically controlled products.

**Kilowatt hours are the units you pay for when you pay your electric bill. Technically, a kilowatt hour is a unit of energy equal to the work done by 1,000 watts in one hour. The cost per kilowatt hour varies in different sections of the country but the national average is about 4.2 cents per kilowatt hour.

Source: Association of Home Appliance Manufacturers (AHAM), 20 North Wacker Drive, Chicago, Ill. 60606.

SESSION 3

Nurture People

Nurture People

An Overview

Simple living "technology" can become so stressed that the important human element is neglected. "As soon as I get the solar-collector built, then I will have time to spend with my family," was a comment I heard recently.

Although every day of this series is a "nurture people day," this session provides a framework to make our caring more apparent. Nurturing people is at the core of living *more* with less. The nurture people day will focus on ourselves, our families, and our friends. During the sessions, we will experience both returning good for good and good for evil, the ultimate goal of the nurturer.

We will try to understand how systems and styles can help or hinder nurturing. Three exercises are described which teach nurturing ways of responding to people. Choose those which seem most suitable for the group:

(1) *An Imaginary Family Vacation* is an enlightening way to observe how families make decisions. Although it may be done playfully, threads of truth will come through.

(2) *Responding to Others* is meant to create awareness of the impact that our language has on others and vice versa. It also is an exercise to practice nurturing.

(3) *Broken Squares*, a puzzle-making exercise, demonstrates the results of systems of competition, cooperation, and autocracy.

Secret Pals or *Friends of St. Nicolas* is a popular event in which gifts, messages, or deeds are performed secretly. Plan carefully so *everyone* who wishes to play both *is* and *has* a secret pal. Otherwise, disappointment can result. During the morning worship or when the parts are assigned, tell the story of St. Nicolas, the model for a secret pal.

A *Stone Soup Cookout* fits well with the theme. Although coordination will be needed, this style of meal depends on everyone participating in preparation of the meal. The story from which the idea came is included.

Caring for ourselves is also part of nurturing. Encourage participants to reflect on their own needs for nurture and what satisfies the need. Care of the body through good nutrition is suggested for a special interest session. Charts and recipes are included.

For the evening, try a talent show with silly skits and serious talent. Summarize the experiences of the day during vespers.

PLAN FOR THE DAY

Biblical References

Ruth 1:1-18 and Luke 10:29-37. The story of loyal friends, Ruth and Naomi, and of the good Samaritan.

Objectives of the Day

1. To give and receive nurture through planned and spontaneous activities.

2. To become aware of systems and styles which promote or discourage nurturing.

Time	Activities and Comments	Equipment and Supplies
15 min.	*Morning worship.* "Going the extra mile." Tell the stories about Ruth and Naomi and/or the Good Samaritan. Have participants close their eyes and imagine themselves as the people in the stories. When did they feel alone or cared for? When do they need nurturing? When do they give it? *Song:* "Make new friends, but keep the old. Some are silver, the others gold."	Bible
15 min.	*Secret pals* or "Friends of St. Nicolas." Have everyone who wants to participate place their name in a box, then draw out the name of someone else who will be their secret pal for the day. During that day, secret pals can make or say or do something for their pal but try not to be discovered. Begin by reading the story of St. Nicolas (not the same as *The Night Before Christmas*). At vespers, develop the service around experiences of the day.	Story of St. Nicolas*

5 min.   *Circular backrubs.* Begin session by forming two circles, one within the other. Have outer circle people rub backs of inner circle people. Switch. Then have inner circle people close eyes and outer circle move a new person and rub their back. Switch. Have participants tell how this felt.

20 min.   *An imaginary family vacation.* An exercise for family groups which demonstrates ways families can work together.   Plan*

15 min.   *Responding to others.* Situations in which pairs practice responding to statements in positive and negative ways.   Plan*

15 min.   *Broken squares.* An exercise which demonstrates the results of cooperation, competition, and autocracy in a group.   Plan*

Poem. "Am I All Alone?" by Judith Mattison.   Poem*

New games. "Stand Up," a game of cooperation. In pairs, sit on ground, back to back, knees bent and elbows linked. The aim is to stand up together. Add a 3rd and 4th person and try to stand up together.
"The Lap Game." Form two circles, one inside the other, with everyone facing toward the center. On signal, everyone in the inner circle should slowly sit on the lap of the person behind. Once they are seated, the person in the back may give the one in

	front a back rub.—From *New Games Book*.	
30 min.	*Film*, "Martin the Cobbler," Billy Budd Films. May be available through church audiovisual library. This is a charming film using a clay animation, based on a folktale by Tolstoy.	Film 16 mm. projector Screen
	Special interest session. Nurturing your body with nutritious food. Have knowledgeable person talk about nutrition. Prepare yogurt or other food.	Charts* Recipe*
90 min.	*Stone soup cookout.* Gather campers around a cookfire and read the story of "Stone Soup." Provide a large pot and ask everyone to prepare a vegetable and add to the pot, after a stone has been put in. Add water, cook until done. Make Bannock or Bread on a Stick and cook over campfire. For dessert, try Peanut-Butter Balls.	Story* Recipes*
	Craft. Make warm fuzzies (yarn balls) to wear around neck or give to someone else.	Yarn
	Evening program. Try a talent show. Have St. Nicolas appear with mitre and robe to talk to his pals.	
	Vespers. "The Story of Barrington Bunny" from *The Way of the Wolf* is provocative for all ages. Martin Bell, Seabury Press, New York, 1968.	

STONE SOUP

Once upon a time in Russia, there was a famine. Little food had been harvested that year because of the lack of rain. During that year, a beggar came into a village carrying a balalaika, a musical instrument like a guitar. The beggar went from house to house, offering to play music in return for food and a place to spend the night. but the villagers hid their food and said that they, too, had nothing to eat and the beggar could not stay there.

So the beggar decided to make stone soup. He built a fire and found a large pot which he filled with water. Into the pot, he placed a large stone. He then sat down and waited for the water to boil. He played beautiful music on his balalaika while he watched the fire.

Curiosity brought the villagers to the pot, and one by one, they suggested that a carrot or potato or some cabbage or barley would add a little gusto to the soup. They ran home and gathered something from their storage cellars and added it to the soup. Soon there was a delicious soup and the villagers stayed to eat with the beggar. The evening continued with singing and dancing while the beggar played music. The beggar was offered a bed for the night.

Recipes for Stone Soup Cookout

Stone Soup: for about 25

To a large pot of boiling water (soap the outside of the pot if you are cooking on an open fire), add one large clean stone and—

3 cups each of:	1 cup each of:	pre-cook and add
onions	noodles	1 cup each of:
carrots	bulgur	lentils
celery	barley	split peas
corn	rice	dried beans
tomatoes		
potatoes	Add to taste: oregano, basil, garlic,	
cabbage	tarragon, salt, and pepper	

Bannock or Bread on a Stick:

Bisquick works best. To one box, add 1 cup dry powdered milk and enough water to make a thick stiff mixture. Wrap around long sticks and hold over an open fire. Cook slowly. Pull off stick when brown. Stuff with cheese or jelly.

Peanut-Butter Balls: about 25

Mix together and form into balls:
3 cups peanut butter
1 cup dry powdered milk
¾ cup honey
½ cup carob powder or cocoa

½ cup of any or all of:
raisins or chopped dried fruits
carob chips, coconut
nuts, chopped
sunflower seeds

ST. NICOLAS

St. Nicolas was born to a rich and noble family in Asia Minor in the third century. His parents died when he was young and he had a lonely life as an orphan. As a young man, he decided to devote his life entirely to the service of God. Obeying the words of Christ, he distributed all his possessions to the poor, the sick, and the suffering.

St. Nicolas is said to have secretly helped poor people by putting gifts of money through their windows or chimneys during the night when no one could see see him or know who was bringing the gift. One night, St. Nicolas threw gold coins in a poor woman's stocking which was hanging by the fire to dry.

This story began a custom of gift-giving in which the giver remained anonymous and no thanks was expected.

AM I ALL ALONE?

By Judith Mattison
Sometimes I feel like I'm the only one
        who drives within the speed limit
        who conserves heat in the winter
        who tries to live with less.
It's no fun.
I can't get much satisfaction
from feeling self-righteous, especially when friends
wear the latest fashions
or buy a new gadget appliance.
I feel alone.

I need support—
friends like me who try,
who have ideas for practical conservation.
I could find them, I'm sure,
if I asked around a bit,
shared my ideas.
I know you support me, Lord.
Lead me to people who care.
—From *Help Me Adapt, Lord,* used by permission.

AN IMAGINARY FAMILY VACATION

An exercise for an intergenerational group.

Purpose

To gain insight into your own family and into yourself through the mirror of another family member or friend.

Time

20 minutes or longer.

Setting

Any place where groups of about six people can be together, yet near the leader to hear instructions.

Instructions

Create "families" by dividing into groups of about six, with children and adults mixed (preferably with nuclear family members together). Explain to the "families" that each person is to pretend that they are a different person in their family, of the opposite sex, and of a different age. For example, a young girl will be an adult man. Have the participants close their eyes to imagine themselves as they will be. Give the "family" time to get reacquainted.

Having identified their new role in their "family," tell them that they are going to take a vacation together. They must first decide where they are going and what they want to do. Allow about 10 minutes for their interaction.

After deciding on where they are going on the vacation, present these (or your own) situations for the "families" to settle:

"The day of vacation has arrived. You are packing the car. There are too many suitcases. No one took the dog to the kennel. What do you do?"

"You are looking for a place to spend the night. Do you go to a motel, to a friend's house (whom you haven't talked to for two years), to a campground? Do you drive all night?"

"Oh, oh, the car breaks down far from any town. And junior isn't feeling well."

"A beautiful day! Let's all do something. Let's—

Keep giving situations until you notice restlessness. Then ask groups to talk about the following:

Did you feel your ideas were important and that others listened to you?
Did you listen to others?
Describe your feeling when you were another different person.
What did you learn from this imaginary vacation?

Note: If you observe that the groups are fighting most of the time, you may want to have a second round in which they model the standard of nurturing people.

RESPONDING TO OTHERS

An exercise for an intergenerational group.

Purpose

To improve your empathy and to practice different ways of responding to others when they speak to you.

Time

15 minutes or longer.

Setting

Anyplace where pairs can be together and hear instructions from leader.

Instructions

There are different ways to respond or talk to someone else. Some ways show the other person we really listened to what they said and we care about their problem and about them. Other ways of responding detract, or take away from what they said. For example, if someone says, "I learned to ride a bicycle today" and the other person answers, "There is dirt on your shirt," the answer would not encourage further conversation or good feelings. On the other hand, the following response encourages and shows caring: "I imagine you worked hard to learn to ride. How did you do it?"

In pairs, have one person make a statement such as suggested below, with his or her own ending. Then have the other person respond, first in a negative way, then positively. Allow them time to talk about their reactions before switching roles. To help get started, you may want to list incomplete sentences, such as:

"One thing I like is...."
"Today I want...."
"I feel sad when...."
"Something which scares me is...."
"I get angry when...."

To wrap up this exercise, bring the group together and ask them what they learned and how they felt about different responses. Hand out "Characteristics of Strong Families."

CHARACTERISTICS OF STRONG (OR HEALTHY) FAMILIES

1. Members frequently and spontaneously show respect, affection, and appreciation for each other.

   > Members feel they matter, are loved, are recognized, are cared about. Avoid taken-for-grantedness.

2. Awareness, acceptance, valuing, and celebration of individual uniquenesses and differences and an absence of rigidity, dominance, and strict hierarchy in family relationships.

   > Creativity and originality rather than mere conformity are emphasized. Democratic in decision making; while parents take strong leadership position, views of all members are invited, encouraged, and considered.

3. Flexible in making adjustments and open to change.

   > Stability and continuity in daily lives, but adaptable enough to modify habits and routines when needed.

4. Communicate easily and well, facing conflicts openly and trying to solve them.

   > Not conflict-free, but face and deal with conflicts. Listen well, share own needs and wants clearly, open about feelings. Waste little energy on blaming and fault-finding.

5. High degree of unity centered around commonly recognized and shared values and goals.

   > Have a core or center of shared values and goals. All members pretty well know what family stands for. Parents continually let children know what they believe in.

6. Members have a strong commitment to one another and do a lot of things together.

   > Busy families. But members are committed to one another's welfare. Make time to do enjoyable things together. Mutual planning.

7. Have "connections" with other families and the community.

   > Not isolated. Involved in community. Have ties with other families with whom they socialize and who can aid them in times of need.

Activity Areas

1. Family communication: Strong families *talk* together.
2. Family council: Strong families *plan* together.

3. Family work: Strong families *work* together.
4. Family recreation: Strong families play together.
5. Families meals: Strong families *dine* together.
6. Family events and celebrations: Strong families develop *rituals.*
7. Family values, religion, and philosophy of life: Strong families share common *values and goals.*
8. Family creativity: Strong families encourage, practice, and enjoy *creative* efforts.
9. Family strengths: Strong families identify and celebrate their *strengths.*

LISTEN!

When I ask you to listen to me and you start giving advice, you have not done what I asked.

When I ask you to listen to me, and you begin to tell me why I should not feel that way, you are trampling on my feelings.

When I ask you to listen to me and you feel you have to do something to solve my problems, you have failed me, strange as that may seem.

Listen! All I asked was to listen to me—not talk or do—just hear me, please.

Advice is cheap. Seventy-five cents can get you both "Dear Abby" and "Billy Graham" in the same newspaper.

And I can do for myself; I am not helpless. Maybe discouraged and faltering, but not helpless.

When you do something for me that I can do and need to do for myself, you contribute to my fear and inadequacy.

But when you accept as a simple fact that I do feel what I feel, no matter how irrational, then I can quit trying to convince you and get about this business of understanding what is behind this irrational feeling.

When that's clear—the answers are obvious and I don't need advice. Irrational feelings make sense when we understand what's behind them.

So, please listen and hear me, and if you want to talk, wait a minute for your turn—I will listen to you.

—Excerpt from "Listen" by Ray Houghton. Used by permission.

BROKEN SQUARES

An exercise for an intergenerational group.

Purpose

To explore the results of cooperation, competition, and strong authority among group members solving a problem.

Time

About 15 minutes.

Setting

Tables or floor space where groups of five members can sit together, but far enough apart from other groups so they cannot see the others' work.

Supplies

Set of puzzles, made out of paper. One set should be provided for each five-member group. If there are six groups, you will need six sets. The pieces will be redistributed among members.

To prepare a set, use square paper, at least 6″ × 6″. Make sure all pieces—a, c and f—are the same size. Draw the lines lightly, then cut each square as follows:

Now, distribute the puzzle pieces into five piles and fasten together with a paper clip, the following way:

Pile 1: pieces a, a, a, c
Pile 2: pieces i, h, e
Pile 3: pieces d, f
Pile 4: pieces g, b, f, c
Pile 5: pieces a, j

Instructions

1. Ask the participants to give examples of situations in which there is competition, cooperation, and a strong authority figure, a boss. Ask them which style they think would complete a puzzle more quickly?

2. Divide into groups of five members each. If there are extra

people, have them be observers. Separate the groups around the room.

3. Tell all the groups together that their goal is to have five completed squares. When they are done, they should raise their hands. While they work, they are not to talk.

4. If there are three groups or multiples of three, designate one or more as competitive, one or more as cooperative, and the others as autocratic.

a. To the competitive group: Tell them that the person in their group who finishes a square first is the "winner."

b. To the cooperative group: Tell them that the group goal of completing five squares is more important than individual goal of completing a square.

c. To the autocratic group: Tell them that the person whose birthday is closest to the day is "boss." The "boss" will give all orders quietly for the completion of five squares.

5. Distribute the five piles of puzzle pieces, one pile to each member of a group, making sure all five piles are given to every group. Tell them not to look at the pieces until a signal is given.

6. Give the signal to begin. The groups are to work until all of them have completed the puzzles.

7. When all are completed, take a few minutes to talk about the process. Ask observers what they saw. Ask participants if they were surprised by the outcome. Ask them how they felt during the process. As a leader, explain that there are situations in which all three styles are appropriate, but it is important to know why and the alternatives. Ask them for examples of when the styles are useful.

LET'S MAKE YOGURT

Objective

The children will use a yogurt culture to convert milk into yogurt.

Materials

First day:

Crock or earthenware bowl (1½ quart size)
Measuring spoon
Stirring spoon
Saucepan

Thermometer (optional)
Skimmed milk—1 quart
Culture—4 tablespoons plain yogurt (containing live culture)

Second day:

Small cups and spoons for everyone present
Honey and/or fruit in bowls for serving with yogurt

Procedure

1. Heat milk until warm but not boiling (110°F.)

   Pour into crock or earthenware bowl.

   Cool until a little warmer than lukewarm (test by putting a drop on inside part of wrist; the milk should feel warm but not hot).

   Add yogurt culture (which should be at room temperature) and blend into bowl.

   Cover bowl and cover completely with a warm blanket or in a turned-off oven. Let stand for at least seven hours or overnight at room temperature.

   Place in refrigerator.

   The next day put a small amount, about a teaspoon, of yogurt in cups.

   Taste yogurt plain.

   Encourage the children to try more yogurt with fruit or honey.

2. Discuss the change in *form* from a liquid to a solid.

   Taste: Sweet to sour

   Consistency: Thin to thick

3. Older children may discuss which countries use yogurt extensively, why they use it and how it originated.*

Teacher's Note

An alternative method: combine skim milk (made from powdered milk) with evaporated milk to make yogurt. Reconstitute both according to instruction on can or package. Use about two thirds skim milk to one third evaporated. For one quart, use three cups reconstituted evaporated milk plus four additional tablespoons of powdered milk. Proceed as with skimmed milk.

U.S. DIETARY GOALS

1. To avoid overweight, consume only as much energy (calories) as is expended; if overweight, decrease energy intake and increase energy expenditure.

2. Increase the consumption of complex carbohydrates and "naturally occurring" sugars from about 28 percent of energy intake to about 48 percent of energy intake.

3. Reduce the consumption of refined and processed sugars by

---

*Yogurt and cheese are ways of preserving milk. Reprinted by permission from *Creative Food Experiences for Children*, available from the Center for Science in the Public Interest, 1755 S St., N.W., Washington, DC 20009, copyright 1980.

Examples of Complementary Proteins

Combinations	Recipes
1. Rice + Legumes	Baked Split Peas
	Hopping John
	Roman Rice and Beans
	Crusty Soybean Casserole
2. Rice + Wheat + Soy	Mexican Grains
3. Rice + Sesame Seed	Sesame Vegetable Rice
4. Rice + Milk	Con Queso Rice
	Spanish Rice Au Gratin
	Spinach Casserole
5. Wheat Products + Milk	Lasagna
	Cheese Fondue
	Macaroni and Cheese
6. Cornmeal + Beans	Mexican Pan Bread
	Pinto Bean Pie
7. Beans + Milk	Bean Chowder
8. Wheat + Beans	Taboulli
9. Peanuts + Milk + Wheat	Peanut-Butter Sandwich and Milk

about 45 percent to account for about 10 percent of total energy intake.

    4. Reduce overall fat consumption from approximately 40 percent to about 30 percent of energy intake.

    5. Reduce saturated fat consumption to account for about 10 percent of total energy intake; and balance that with poly-unsaturated and mono-unsaturated fats, which should account for about 10 percent of energy intake each.

    6. Reduce cholesterol consumption to about 300 mg. a day.

    7. Limit the intake of sodium by reducing the intake of salt to about five grams a day.

The Goals Suggest the Following Changes in Food Selection and Preparation:

    1. Increase consumption of fruits and vegetables and whole grains.

    2. Decrease consumption of refined and other processed sugars and foods high in such sugars.

    3. Decrease consumption of foods high in total fat, and partially replace saturated fats, whether obtained from animal or vegetable

sources, with poly-unsaturated fats.

4. Decrease consumption of animal fat, and choose meats, poultry, and fish which will reduce saturated fat intake.

5. Except for young children, substitute low-fat and non-fat milk for whole milk, and low-fat dairy products for high-fat dairy products.

6. Decrease consumption of butterfat, eggs, and other high cholestrol sources. Some consideration should be given to easing the cholesterol goal for pre-menopausal women, young children, and the elderly in order to obtain the nutritional benefits of eggs in the diet.

7. Decrease consumption of foods high in salt content.

Persons with physical and/or mental ailments who have reason to believe that they should not follow guidelines for the general population should consult with a health professional having expertise in nutrition, regarding their individual case.

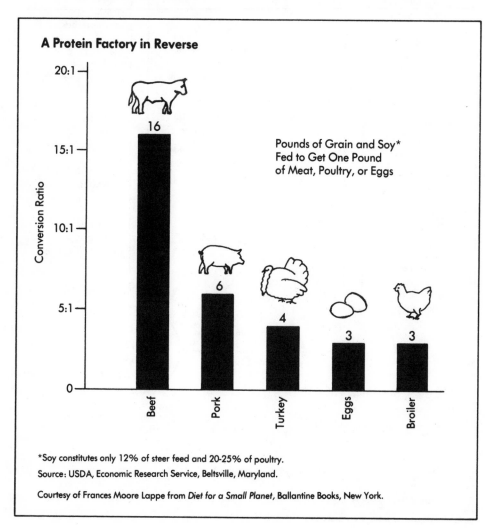

A Protein Factory in Reverse

Conversion Ratio

Pounds of Grain and Soy*
Fed to Get One Pound
of Meat, Poultry, or Eggs

Beef — 16
Pork — 6
Turkey — 4
Eggs — 3
Broiler — 3

*Soy constitutes only 12% of steer feed and 20-25% of poultry.

Source: USDA, Economic Research Service, Beltsville, Maryland.

Courtesy of Frances Moore Lappe from *Diet for a Small Planet*, Ballantine Books, New York.

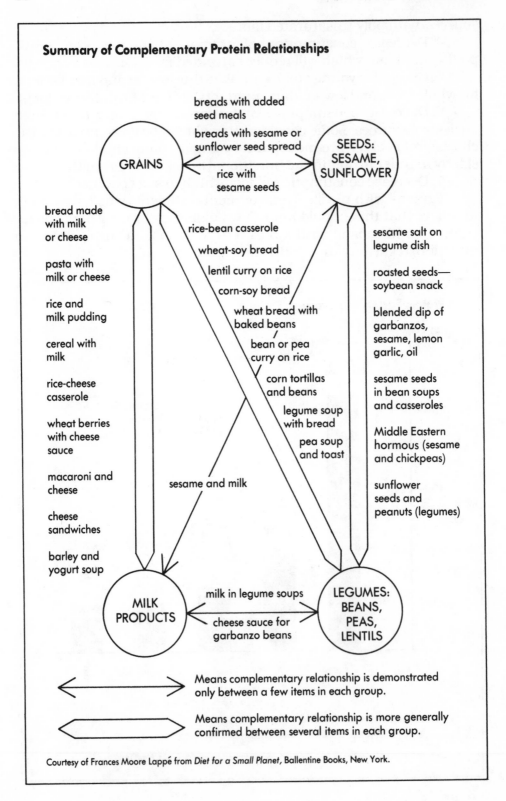

Summary of Complementary Protein Relationships

GRAINS

SEEDS: SESAME, SUNFLOWER

MILK PRODUCTS

LEGUMES: BEANS, PEAS, LENTILS

breads with added seed meals

breads with sesame or sunflower seed spread

rice with sesame seeds

bread made with milk or cheese

pasta with milk or cheese

rice and milk pudding

cereal with milk

rice-cheese casserole

wheat berries with cheese sauce

macaroni and cheese

cheese sandwiches

barley and yogurt soup

rice-bean casserole

wheat-soy bread

lentil curry on rice

corn-soy bread

wheat bread with baked beans

bean or pea curry on rice

corn tortillas and beans

legume soup with bread

pea soup and toast

sesame and milk

sesame salt on legume dish

roasted seeds— soybean snack

blended dip of garbanzos, sesame, lemon garlic, oil

sesame seeds in bean soups and casseroles

Middle Eastern hormous (sesame and chickpeas)

sunflower seeds and peanuts (legumes)

milk in legume soups

cheese sauce for garbanzo beans

Means complementary relationship is demonstrated only between a few items in each group.

Means complementary relationship is more generally confirmed between several items in each group.

Courtesy of Frances Moore Lappé from *Diet for a Small Planet*, Ballentine Books, New York.

SESSION 4

Do
Justice

Do Justice

An Overview

It is necessary to understand our global connections to realize the impact our lives have on people in the rest of the world. In the foreword to *Living More with Less,* Doris Longacre links the small decisions of our lives to complex systems in the world. She states that in North America 6 percent of the world's population use 40 percent of the world's resources. "That way of living makes other people poor," she says.

North Americans have money and power to establish control over the world's energy and food. Many of our luxury goods and bargains are available to us at the expense of other people's energy and food. Furthermore, military expenditures have risen rapidly to protect our access to energy, food, and other resources.

On your Do Justice Day, the global connection theme of learning from the world community will be background to gaining an understanding of justice. *The content can be overwhelming to participants, so it is important to provide ideas and methods of responding so participants don't feel hopeless.*

Dorothy Day, founder of the Catholic Worker movement, devoted her life to serving others and working for justice. When she was asked if she ever became discouraged, she replied, "I wasn't called to be successful, only faithful." Invite participants to make a commitment to this long and sometimes lonely journey.

For the morning worship, a parable, "Ambulance Drivers or Tunnel Builders," is suggested plus "What'er You Do," which can be sung or used as a reading. Reflect on charity and justice, and the need for both at times.

It is important for all participants to understand the concept of justice and how it differs from charity. To do this, help participants build a definition of justice. Start with basic human needs and rights, such as food, shelter, clothing, health care, skills development, and work as basic components of justice. Justice is reflected in the opportunity people have or do not have to possess an equitable share of the world's goods. But justice is more than wants and basic needs being filled. Justice is when people are free to determine their own destinies. It is a synonym for power in their own lives.

After formulating a definition, it is important to understand how the small decisions of our lives are linked to the complex systems in the world which cause injustice. To demonstrate our global connections, ask the group to trace from where the food of the previous day came. What products were locally grown? Which were produced in the United States? Where were the others from? Were there bananas from Honduras, cereal made with palm oil from Malaysia, sugar from the Dominican Republic, coffee from Colombia, fruits from Mexico? Now have them look around. Where did their clothing come from? Check the labels. What about the room's furnishings? Use a map to make the linkages and list the countries. Are there a preponderance of "poor" countries listed? Were these products secured at the expense of poor people working for low wages in indecent conditions?

From this illustration, it is obvious that we are, one and all, globally connected and within this interdependence there are many questions of justice.

The *Bread and People* exercise helps the concept of justice become more real. Allow the participants to talk freely and interact and feel powerful or powerless during the exercise. The teacher/preacher may gather information from this session for a meditation. After this exercise, take action! Write a letter (as a total group or as families) to a leader, such as the President, on an issue which has emerged. The *Bread for the World Guide to Effective Letter Writing* is included for instruction and as an example. For background information, use *Bread for the World* or *Impact* newsletter.*

A mini-drama on the International Year of the Child is included, which can be used during an evening program or whenever it fits. Be sure to allow time for discussion.

A craft project, the making of origami paper cranes, is a symbol for justice. The true story of Sadako is included. By making the cranes, your group is in solidarity with millions of people throughout the world who suffer with the victims of the A-bomb in Japan.

A suggestion for an audiovisual is *The Glass House.* It is an allegory about wealth and poverty, justice, and charity. Because of its style, it is appropriate for all ages.

A special interest session on food co-ops fits the justice theme well. If there is a co-op close by, visit it; otherwise, have samples of kinds of products available, and an explanation of methods of preparation, and time to make something. Shopping in a co-op can be looked at as a step toward justice because all members participate in decision making. The power is equal.

---

*Bread for the World Newsletter, 6411 Chillum Place, N.W., Washington, DC 20012; *Impact Newsletter,* 110 Maryland Avenue, N.E., Washington, DC 20002. Tel. (800) 424-7292.

PLAN FOR THE DAY

Biblical Reference

Micah 6:8. The Lord asks you to act justly, to love tenderly, and to walk humbly with your God.

Objectives of the Day

1. To understand the concept and reality of justice.
2. To do an act of justice and feel a sense of solidarity with others in doing this.

Time	Activities and Comments	Equipment and Supplies
15 min.	*Morning worship.* Read or paraphrase the story "Ambulance Drivers or Tunnel Builders?" Develop a definition of justice. Write on newsprint and post for referral during the day. For background, read *Bread and Justice* by James and Kathleen McGinnis, Paulist Press, 1979.	Story* Marker and newsprint
	Songs: "Dona Nobis Pacem" (Give Us Peace); "May There Always Be Sunshine"	Songs*
20 min.	*Bread and People,* a simulation on distribution of food and people in the world. This could be used at worship.	Plan and litany* Map of world Uncut loaf of bread
15 min.	*An act of justice.* Write letters of concern, encouragement, or praise to elected officials. Youngsters can write their own, or work together on a group letter and have everyone sign or add a remark. *Impact* and *Bread for the World* have background papers on	Stationery and pens Stamps "Guide to Effective Letter Writing" from *Bread for the World** Names and addresses of elected officials

	many issues. Collect letters during a worship time as an offering.	*BFW Newsletter* *IMPACT Newsletter*
20 min.	*Film,* "The Glass House" (12 min.), available from many church audiovisual libraries or Augsburg Film Libraries. An allegory about wealth and poverty, justice and charity. Excellent for all ages.	Film 16 mm projector Screen
25 min.	*Story and craft.* The true story of Sadako and the thousand paper cranes she attempted to make as she was dying from radiation sickness in Hiroshima. Instructions for making paper crane is included. Hang the cranes for remembrance and decoration.	Story and instructions* Origami paper or light-weight colored paper, 6″ × 6″ or 9″ × 9″
15 min.	*Mini-drama* of International Year of the Child. Can be read with little preparation. Save a few minutes for reactions.	Mini-drama*
	Special interest group. Talk about shopping in a food co-op or visit one if convenient. Otherwise, have examples of products. Make snacks of food produced locally and explain how this contributes to justice. See *Diet for a Small Planet,* by F. M. Lappé.	
	Vespers. "How Grateful We Are"	Psalm*

WHATE'ER YOU DO
By Marion Lucciola and Patti Sprinkle

Tune: Faith of Our Fathers

1. When I was hungry, you offered me food,
   When I was thirsty, you gave me drink,
   When I was stranger, you opened your door,
   When I was naked, your coat I wore.

Chorus: Whate'er you do to the least of these,
          What you have done, you've done to me.

2. I was imprisoned, you came to my cell,
   Stood by my bedside when I lay ill,
   Though I disguised it, you still knew my face,
   Now come, oh bless-ed, claim your right place!

—Reprinted with permission from *HUNGER: Understanding the Crisis Through Games, Dramas, and Songs,* by Patricia Houck Sprinkle, copyright John Knox Press, 1980.

PSALM OF PRAISE
By Leslie Brandt

How grateful we are, O God,
     for our great country,
     for the blessings You lavish upon our land!
How concerned we are, O God,
     that our very nation may become our god
     and that we worship the gifts
          rather than the Giver!

Is it possible, O God,
     that our laws may circumvent your will?
     that our freedom may place chains on others?
     that our wealth impoverish someone?
     that our power may come
          by way of another's weakness?
     that our enemies may be those
          who are obedient to you?
Dare we pray, O God,
     that you take away those things that come
          between us and you?

that you raise up men who will oppose
> those institutions and those citizens
> > who carelessly, even unconsciously,
> equate patriotism with allegiance to you?

We do pray, O God,
> that our nation be restored to Your objectives
> and that Your children who abide in this land
> > dedicate their lives to You and Your
> > > purposes.

—Used by permission from *Psalms/Now*, copyright 1973 by Concordia Publishing House.

AMBULANCE DRIVERS OR TUNNEL BUILDERS?

By Ronald J. Sider

A group of devout Christians once lived in a small village at the foot of a mountain. A winding, slippery road with hairpin curves and steep precipices without guard rails wound its way up one side of the mountain and down the other. There were frequent fatal accidents. Deeply saddened by the injured people who were pulled from the wrecked cars, the Christians in the village's three churches decided to act. They pooled their resources and purchased an ambulance. Over the years, they saved many lives although some victims remained crippled for life.

Then one day a visitor came to town. Puzzled, he asked why they did not close the road over the mountain and build a tunnel instead. Startled at first, the ambulance volunteers quickly pointed out that this approach (although technically quite possible) was not realistic or advisable. After all, the narrow mountain road had been there for a long time. Besides, the mayor of the town would bitterly oppose the idea. (He owned a large restaurant and service station halfway up the mountain.)

The visitor was shocked that the mayor's economic interests mattered more to these Christians than the many human casualties. Somewhat hesitantly, he suggested that perhaps the churches ought to speak to the mayor. Perhaps they should even elect a different mayor if he proved stubborn and unconcerned. Now the Christians were shocked. With rising indignation and righteous conviction they informed the young radical that the church dare not become involved in politics. The church is called to preach the gospel and give a cup of cold water. Its mission is not to dabble in worldly things like social and political structures.

Perplexed and bitter, the visitor left. As he wandered out of the

village, one question churned round and round in his muddled mind. Is it really more spiritual, he wondered, to operate the ambulances which pick up the bloody victims of destructive social structures than to try to change the structures themselves?
—Used by permission.

BREAD AND PEOPLE
A simulation on population and food distribution.

Purpose

To demonstrate, in a simple way, the relationship between distribution of people and food in the global setting.

Time

20 to 25 minutes.

Setting

Large area where five groups can assemble and talk and still hear leader.

Materials

Map of world.
Large uncut loaf of bread. (French bread works well.) Copies of litany for participants.

Instructions

1. On the world map, point out the five largest continents. Divide the group into these continents by percentage of population (see chart below). Explain that most of the people living where they do were born there and that they did not choose where to be born, just as we did not have that choice.

2. Hold up the loaf of uncut bread and explain that it represents *all* the food which will be eaten today in the world. Then divide the loaf according to the percentages eaten on the five continents and hand the pieces to one person in each group.

3. Hand out the "Sharing Food in a Hungry World" litany (page 89) and read, with continents responding.

4. Instruct the five continents to "feed their people." They might give the same size portion to everyone, or be more realistic and give larger pieces to the ones who are deemed rich and no bread to some, the poor. Continents without much bread may try to get bread from others. Encourage discussion within and between continents. Tell them not to eat the bread until after the simulation. You can make

the game more complex by giving cards with names of resources and products from the continents written on them for trade, or let them think of products and resources from the continents.

5. End by asking all participants to hold up their piece of bread. Point out that the actions and feelings which were happening in the simulation are also happening in the continents. There may be positive happenings in Asia, for example, such as a sense of community in their struggle. End with discussion. The teacher/preacher may find ideas from the simulation for a wrap-up of the session.

Population/food/trade chart for simulation:

Continent	% of People	% of Food	Trade commodities
Africa	10	8	Cocoa, coffee, uranium
Asia	59	23	Jute, bamboo, clothing
Europe	17	36	Watches, wine
South America	8	11	Tin, bananas, coffee
North America	6	22	Weapons, food

A GUIDE TO EFFECTIVE LETTER WRITING ON HUNGER ISSUES

Only one out of every 10 U.S. citizens ever writes a letter to his or her congressional representative, senator, or to the President. The other nine remain silent for reasons such as "congresspersons don't read their mail" and "one letter won't make any difference anyway." The experience of Bread for the World has proved these notions incorrect.

In fact, mail is more important to today's congressperson than ever before. The issues a legislator deals with continue to increase both in complexity and sheer number. And unlike members of Congress in the days of Calhoun, Webster, and Lincoln, our legislators rarely spend more than 60 days a year in their home states and often go to Washington representing 10 times more people than their predecessors.

Congresspersons are the first to acknowledge the increasingly important role played by letters from their constituents:

My mailbag is my best 'hotline' to the people back home. On several occasions a single, thoughtful, factually persuasive letter did change my mind....

Morris Udall
Representative from Arizona

Someone who sits down and writes a letter about hunger ... almost literally has to be saving a life....

Paul Simon
Representative from Illinois

One representative even takes letters with him to the House and then decides which way to vote.

Bread for the World is a grass-roots lobbying movement that uses letters as the primary tool in shaping legislation. For example, an estimated 250,000 letters were generated in support of the Right-to-Food bill. As a result, this resolution was voted out of the committee where it had been held up and was passed by both the Senate and the House.

Rules of Thumb

Obviously, not every letter will change public policy, but one that is well-written is more apt to interest, encourage, and motivate your representatives. Use the guidelines that follow when applicable. No letter will necessarily contain all the suggested elements.

- Be reasonably brief. Rarely should a letter exceed one full page.
- Write your own views in your own words. Little attention is given to a letter which looks like the product of a mail campaign.
- Use stationery with a letterhead, if possible. Be certain your address is on the letter as well as the envelope. Write legibly and spell names correctly.
- Ask for a specific legislative action. Concentrate on one issue per letter. Don't make a shopping list.
- Be considerate. Keep in mind the constraints of the legislative process and the desires of other constituents. Don't threaten or demand; request your representatives' consideration of your views.
- Be constructive. If a bill addresses a legitimate problem but proposes the wrong solution, express this and then go on to give your view as to the correct approach.
- Make your letter timely. Write soon after the bill is introduced to alert your representative to its existence. Write just prior to subcommittee hearings or full committee and floor votes to suggest appropriate action.
- Target your letters. Find out what committees and subcommittees your representatives serve on. Letters to members of a committee considering a bill are often most important. An estimated 90 percent of the bills pass on the floor in the same form that they come from committee.
- Act as a resource person. On occasion, you will be writing on a subject about which you have greater knowledge or access to information than your representative. Share such information by sending

background papers and newspaper articles.

●Consult your BFW monthly newsletter. You will find the numbers and descriptions of bills and updates on their progress in the legislative process.

●Thank your representatives and their legislative aides when you approve of their actions. Statements of disappointment and hopes for future support should also be expressed.

Alternative Means of Communication

Publicize the positions, favorable and unfavorable that your legislators have taken. This can involve many forms of public discussion and education such as letters to your local newspapers, discussion in your church groups and community forums. You can order a Media Kit from Bread for the World that will help you in doing publicity.

Writing a letter is the first step in building an ongoing relationship with your representatives and fulfilling your responsibility as a citizen. The next steps are:

Sending a Telegram. This is a good attention-getter, especially right before a key vote. They are usually counted simply for and against, so make them brief, concise and include the bill number.

Western Union Personal Opinion Messages, which can be sent only to elected officials, have a 40-word limit, are delivered to the White House or Congress within two hours, and cost only $4.25. Mailgrams are delivered the next day, may contain up to 50 words and cost $4.25. The next 50 words cost only $1.95.

Making a Telephone Call. This is the most effective prior to any votes and also offers the possibility of engaging in a dialgoue. Dial (202) 224-3121 to reach any representative or senator in his/her Washington office. If it is not possible to speak directly with your congressperson, ask to speak to the legislative assistant (L.A.) who handles the legislation you are concerned about.

Making a Personal Visit. This is the most effective means of contact. A visit can be arranged for the local or Washington office. Write or phone in advance requesting an appointment. Specify what you wish to discuss. You can contact your Bread for the World regional coordinator in the Washington office if you wish help in planning your visit or reviewing issues.

Arrive prepared. State your views and the action you desire. Seek an expression for or against your position. If you expect to share the results of the meeting with others, including the press, make this clear.

Follow the visit with a letter of appreciation, briefly restating your position and any commitments made at the time of your visit.

Suggested Format

President.......
The White House
Washington, DC 20501

Representative.......
House Office Building
Washington, DC 20515

Senator.......
Senate Office Building
Washington, DC 20510

Dear Senator....:

Dear Representative....:

Dear President....:

Begin with a commendation on a past vote or speech.

Identify the legislation clearly. Give the bill number (and title and author if known) and the stage of the bill in the legislative process. Do not assume the legislator will know the bill you are writing about.

State your reason for writing. Personal experience is the best supporting evidence. Explain what effect the bill will have on you, your community, or your state. If available, offer documented evidence or statistics in support of your views.

Raise questions; they are more likely to encourage a response. The more challenging your letter, the better chance of reaching someone of influence, thus avoiding a routine response or form letter.

Thank you for your consideration of my views.

Sincerely

A Concerned Citizen

789 Tenth Avenue
New York, NY 10010

Senator Daniel P. Moynihan
Senate Office Building
Washington, D.C. 20510

Dear Senator Moynihan:

Congratulations on your remarks on the "Meet the Press" television program of May 21, 1978, regarding world food production and global hunger.

As you may be aware, the proposed international Development Cooperation Act of 1978 (S2420), which would overhaul the U.S. aid program, appears to be stalled in the Senate. This bill would provide an opportunity to rewrite U.S. food and development assistance policy for the first time since 1961.

Present legislation needs clarification of purpose, stability of supplies, and reorganization of its administration. S2420 would, among other things, put all forms of food and developmental assistance under one new agency, thus improving coordination of the programs. It would also enable the new agency and its director to represent global hunger and poverty concerns in the administration when U.S. economic and foreign policy is hammered out.

Do you not agree that the reorganizing of U.S. food and development assistance programs would be an important factor in overcoming hunger in the world?

I urge you to sponsor this bill (S2420) and to encourage the appropriate committees to use it as a framework for rewriting our assistance programs.

Sincerely,

Jane Haskins

Xavier High School
30 West 16th Street
New York, NY 10011

Representative S. William Green
House of Representatives
Washington, D.C. 20515

Dear Representative Green:
I have noticed that you have continually supported the positions taken by Bread for the World. I want you to know that at least this constituent is impressed by this fact and that I appreciate your expressed concern for the eventual solution to the problem of world hunger.

Sincerely yours,

J. F. Donnelly, S.J.

1901 Arlington Road, S.W.
Roanoke, VA 24015

Representative M. Caldwell Butler
House of Representatives
Washington, D.C. 20515

Dear Representative Butler:

While I realize that you are not a member of either the House Agriculture Committee or the House Foreign Affairs Committee, I am writing asking that you support the movement of the Food Security Act (HR 3611/12) out of committee into final passage.

The passage of this legislation would not only serve to establish a food reserve needed as protection against famine caused by natural disaster, but it would provide a stable base for the use of grain purchased by the United States government as a result of the cancellation of grain contracts with Russia. Passage of this legislation at this time would be both morally and economically sound.

Any attention you can give to this matter will be deeply appreciated.

Sincerely,
William E. Pauley

—This guide was prepared by Bread for the World, a Christian citizens lobbying organization concerned with legislation that will alleviate domestic and world hunger. For more information, write: Bread for the World, 6411 Chillum Place NW, Washington, DC 20012. Reprinted by permission.

THE PEACE CRANE

A Japanese tradition holds that anyone who folds one thousand paper cranes will have a fervently held desire fulfilled.

Sadako Sasaki was a young girl when the atom bomb exploded over Hiroshima in 1945. Ten years later, after a lifetime of normal health, she fell ill with radiation sickness. Her remaining days were spent in a hospital.

From her bed, Sadako set out to fold a thousand paper cranes as a prayer for peace. At first it was easy enough, but as the illness grew worse each fold became an immense labor. When she died in 1956 she had been able to complete only 644. From her deathbed she held up one crane and said in a quiet voice, "I will write peace on your wings and you will fly all over the world." Others took up her unfinished task.

Since her death millions upon millions of paper cranes have been folded, especially by the children of Japan. Beginning in 1958, on Children's Day (May 5), they have come from all parts of Japan to Hiroshima's Peace Park bringing blizzards of paper cranes up to the tower where a statue of a young girl who died in the bombing stands surrounded by these folded paper prayers. The children mourn the deaths of the atom bomb's victims—still continuing to die of radiation illness three decades after the blast—and vow to join the *hibakusha* (survivors of atomic war) in building a world that will choose the way of peace. At the foot of the Hiroshima tower, in the midst of the paper cranes, the words are carved: THIS IS OUR CRY, THIS IS OUR PRAYER: TO ESTABLISH PEACE IN THE WORLD.

On the following pages are directions for making origami cranes.

JAPANESE PEACE CRANES

USE LIGHTWEIGHT PAPER OR SPECIAL ORIGAMI PAPER, CUT IN EXACT SQUARE, 6" × 6" OR 9" × 9". MAKE ALL FOLDS EXACT AND CREASE EACH FOLD SHARPLY.

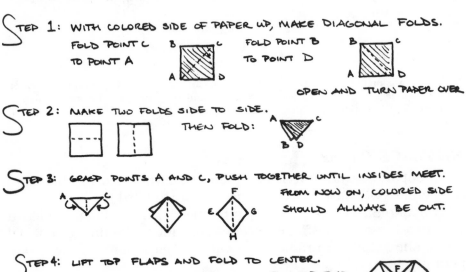

STEP 1: WITH COLORED SIDE OF PAPER UP, MAKE DIAGONAL FOLDS. FOLD POINT C TO POINT A   FOLD POINT B TO POINT D
OPEN AND TURN PAPER OVER

STEP 2: MAKE TWO FOLDS SIDE TO SIDE. THEN FOLD:

STEP 3: GRASP POINTS A AND C, PUSH TOGETHER UNTIL INSIDES MEET. FROM NOW ON, COLORED SIDE SHOULD ALWAYS BE OUT.

STEP 4: LIFT TOP FLAPS AND FOLD TO CENTER. FOLD TOP FLAP DOWN.

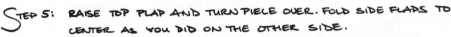

STEP 5: RAISE TOP FLAP AND TURN PIECE OVER. FOLD SIDE FLAPS TO CENTER AS YOU DID ON THE OTHER SIDE.

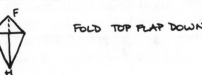

FOLD TOP FLAP DOWN:

OPEN ALL FLAPS, TOP, BACK, FRONT, BACK AND YOU ARE BACK TO WHERE YOU WERE IN STEP 3.

STEP 6: RAISE TOP LAYER OF PAPER AND PULL ALL THE WAY UP AND BACK.

 FLATTEN:

TURN OVER AND DO THE SAME TO OTHER SIDE.

STEP 7: FOLD SIDE A SO IT LIES ALONG CENTER. THEN, DO THE SAME TO SIDE B.

 SIDE A

SIDE B SIDE A SPLIT

TURN OVER AND DO THE SAME ON THE OTHER TWO SIDES:

STEP 8: FOLD ONE "LEG" BACK AND THEN FORWARD ON THE SAME LINE. REVERSE FOLD THE INSIDE OF THE LEG.

DO THE SAME WITH THE OTHER LEG:

 WINGS HEAD

STEP 9: FINISH HEAD BY CREASING FORWARD AND BACK, MAKING A REVERSE FOLD.

 CREASE BOTH INSIDE AND OUT

PUSH INSIDE OUT.

STEP 10: GRASP TIPS OF WINGS AND GENTLY PULL APART. YOU CAN ALSO BLOW IN HOLE UNDERNEATH TO PUFF BODY.

WRITE "PEACE," OR "PAX" ON WINGS.

TO HANG THE CRANES, USING THREAD WITH NEEDLE, GO UP THROUGH THE BODY. PLACE ONE CRANE ON TOP OF THE OTHER IN A LONG LINE.

Lettered and illustrated by Michael J. Dregni.

May There Always Be Sunshine!

L. Oshanina*   SOVIET CHILDREN'S PEACE SONG   Music by A. Ostrovshova

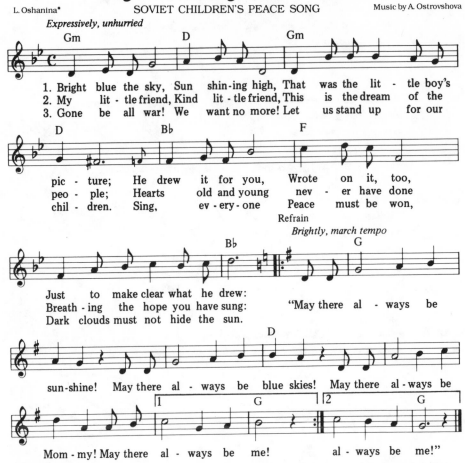

1. Bright blue the sky, Sun shin-ing high, That was the lit - tle boy's
2. My lit - tle friend, Kind lit - tle friend, This is the dream of the
3. Gone be all war! We want no more! Let us stand up for our

pic - ture; He drew it for you, Wrote on it, too,
peo - ple; Hearts old and young nev - er have done
chil - dren. Sing, ev - ery - one Peace must be won,

Just to make clear what he drew:
Breath - ing the hope you have sung: "May there al - ways be
Dark clouds must not hide the sun.

sun-shine! May there al - ways be blue skies! May there al - ways be

Mom - my! May there al - ways be me!   al - ways be me!"

*Author of the original Russian text; English text (from Russian) anonymous. Courtesy of Phyllis Sanders and WILPF © 1964, CRS, Inc., transferred to World Around Songs, Inc., 1979. Used by permission.

Dona Nobis Pacem

Source Unknown   3-part Canon

Do - na no - bis pa - cem, pa-cem, do - na no - bis pa - cem.

Do - na no - bis pa-cem; do - na no - bis pa - cem.

Do - na no - bis pa - cem; do - na no - bis pa - cem.

Translation: Give to us peace.

OUR CHILDREN
A One-Act Play

CAST: NARRATOR
MS. BERTHA COLDHEART
MS. WANDA WARMHEART

Narrator: *THE SITUATION*
The International Year of the Child is over! Everyone got so excited. Who did not respond with *sympathy* to the picture of the forlorn, starving waif? Concern for children is always a safe issue—or is it?

THE SETTING
Shady Side Country Club in Sliding Slope, California; the Wednesday pre-prayer meeting bridge club. Ms. Wanda Warmheart and Ms. Bertha Coldheart are enjoying a break while Miss Sally Lilly and her partner Miss Kinda Dummy, having just gone down six on a seven heart contract, are in the powder room recovering.

Ms. Coldheart: Wasn't Sally silly for bidding seven hearts after I had already bid six hearts?

Ms. Warmheart: Sally's always silly—but speaking of hearts, don't those posters still in the lobby of those pitiful children for the International Year of the Child exhibit sadden your heart?

Ms. Coldheart: No! It upsets me! Why don't they take them down? Why should they spoil the one place where we can get away from all the problems of the world? Besides, I think it's obscene. Why do they always use pictures like that to try to make us feel guilty when they ask for more money!

Ms. Warmheart: Sorry I mentioned it, Bertha. I forgot about your blood pressure.

Ms. Coldheart: Sorry! Ha! I always knew you were one of those phony liberals. I have never liked the United Nations, and this was a plot of theirs to make us help children in communist countries where they spend all their money on weapons and where they don't care about people anyway!

Ms. Warmheart: Now, Bertha—I think you have it all wrong! The I.Y.C. program asked countries to look at *their own* children, their welfare, their *rights* as children. Around the world "a slaughter of innocents" continues, but we don't even see the problem at home. What about children in America? What did we really do for them?

Ms. Coldheart: Oh, Wanda, now you're being sillier than Sally. Children in our country don't need rights. We all take good care of our children. Mine are in the best boarding schools in the East.

Ms. Warmheart: Oh!

Ms. Coldheart: Oh! Oh look, we have more important things to be concerned about—inflation, energy, security. I'm glad we passed Proposition 13, but the energy shortage is bound to increase because of those anti-nuclear radicals. And think of those who want to cut down in our military spending. The President just had to cut health and human services programs to keep us strong! Those are the real issues—not children!

Ms. Warmheart: Now, Bertha! You listen! Don't you think those issues affect the lives of our children? But, those are not the only things that we have to be concerned about. Haven't you heard about child abuse or child pornography? Even with the International Year of the Child, the basic facts did not change. Ten million kids in our country receive no regular health care, a third have never seen a dentist, 20 million kids are not protected from the major childhood diseases. We have an embarrassingly high infant mortality rate; and these conditions are worse among blacks and minorities....

Ms. Coldheart: *(Defensively)* But my maid has never complained about her kids.

Ms. Warmheart: Dear God! How can I get her to understand?

Narrator: Can you help Wanda Warmheart? Do children have rights? What are the responsibilities of the government of a democratic people for the welfare of its people? What is the role of the church? What trade-offs are we making regarding our children? What are the implications that *two thirds* of the people in the United States that are on welfare are children?!

—Reprinted by permission from *The Book of Five Acts* or "How to Struggle with Justice Issues Painlessly," by Robert F. Smylie, 1980.

SHARING FOOD IN A HUNGRY WORLD

Leader: The earth is the Lord's. The Lord created the world and all who dwell therein.

All people representing continents: We are the people of the major continents of the world. We love life and offer praise to the Lord of our lives. Let every kindred, every tribe on this terrestrial ball, to God all majesty ascribe and crown Lord of all.

Leader: Praise be to God, the Lord of all the peoples of the earth.

Africa: We are a country filled with beauty and promise, pain and poverty. We yearn to be free.

Asia: Burdened with masses of hungry people, we cry for the bread of heaven and the bread of earth.

Europe: Once mighty in the eyes of all the world, and now the most densely populated of the continents, we seek economic stability.

Latin America: Rapidly growing in people and poverty, we look to our neighbors to the north, east, and west.

North America: We are on top of the world. We possess many things, and yet we are anxious about our dependence upon the exports of the rest of the world to maintain our consumptive lifestyle.

All people representing continents: Praise be to God, the Lord of all the peoples of the earth.

Leader: How did you get where you are? By choice? No, by chance. This is true of the inhabitants of the world. How many of you are there on your continent?

Africa: Ten percent of the people.

Asia: Fifty-nine percent of the people.

Europe: Seventeen percent of the people.

Latin America: Eight percent of the people.

North America: Six percent of the people.

Leader: Do your people earn enough to have enough to eat, to live well?

Africa: Our 10 percent of the world's people eat 8 percent of the world's food.

Asia: Our 59 percent of the world's people eat 23 percent of the world's food.

Europe: Our 17 percent of the world's people eat 36 percent of the world's food.

Latin America: Our 8 percent of the world's people eat 11 percent of the world's food.

North America: Our 6 percent of the world's people eat 22 percent of the world's food.

Leader: This unequal distribution is the cause of the malnourishment and starvation in God's world and it should be the concern of all Christians. What can we do?

All people: Perhaps the nations that have more than enough food will share with those who don't have enough. Perhaps business can help developing countries solve their own problems by sharing technology and resources. Perhaps churches can give more to help hungry people help themselves. Perhaps we all can make decisions to help our hungry world help itself.

SESSION 5

Nonconform Freely

Nonconform Freely

An Overview

To live seriously the first four life standards means nonconforming to many aspects of American culture. Nonconformity in this session is not about irresponsibility and unusual clothing and "doing your own thing," as the word nonconformity may suggest. It is about resistance to being molded into materialism and destructive cultural trends.

Material goods are necessary to sustain life. Materialism is the condition which results from an addiction to material goods. Jesus never said material things are evil in themselves but they can threaten our freedom. The problem is the *love* of material goods and the hold they can exert over us.

Nonconformity is complicated and a paradox. It frees us to be "as slaves in God's service," says Peter. Nonconformity can also release energy to enrich our lives, to find more meaning, more compatibility with our earth, our neighbor, and with God.

The primary purpose of this session is to become aware of the pressures to conform and consume which dominate our society. With awareness, we can decide what we will allow to influence us and what we can discard. Another purpose is to use the life standards in creative and freeing ways. As our standards or values become more congruent with the actions of our lives we will become more whole as people and as a society.

During the Nonconform Freely Day, the ideas and plans which are included can be carried out with spontaneity. *Pressures to Consume and Conform* include making collages. *What would do if...?* presents situations for role playing which combine nonconformity and the other four life standards.

A pledge of commitment to an action helps participants connect their learning experience with their home situation. Allow ample time for individual or family reflection on the pledge. The presentation of the pledge can be incorporated into the evening celebration or worship. Repeat the lifestyle charades, as done in the first session, but as something they will do in the future.

For the evening, suggest an alternative celebration. Have an "everybody" birthday party or take favorite parts of different traditional celebrations and have an eclectic celebration. Involve everyone in some way with the planning and production of the event, spending part of the afternoon doing this.

During the final gathering, repeat some of the songs and stories of the week. A community has probably been built during the week that will now need to end, but the ties will linger. As a closing exercise for the week, bring the group together in a circle and do a symbolic separation and coming together in spirit. End with passing of the peace and a benediction.

PLAN FOR THE DAY

Biblical Reference

Romans 12:2. Do not be conformed to the world.

Objectives of the Day

1. To gain awareness of pressures in our society to conform and consume.

2. To understand the dynamics of change and the need for support during change.

3. To make a commitment to a specific action during the next week.

Time	Activities and Comments	Equipment and Supplies
15 min.	*Morning worship.* Meditation on the Beatitudes.	Meditation* Bible
	Song: "Simple Gifts" Music is adaptable to instruments and move-ment.	Song*
30 min.	*Filmstrip,* "Consumerland, How High the Mountain?" Argus Communications, 1972. A hu-morous cartoon about advertis-ing pressures.	Filmstrip Filmstrip projector Cassette recorder Screen
30 min.	*Pressures to Consume and Conform,* an exercise to help understand the impact of ad-vertising. Small groups make collages of advertisements.	Plan* Old magazines Paste or tape Newsprint Markers
15-20 min.	*What Would You Do If. . . ?* an exercise of role playing situa-	Plan* Handout or chalk-

tions in which there is nonconformity.

board and chalk

Craft. Try finger painting or sand painting on surface of glue.

An alternative celebration. Plan and enjoy a celebration which combines the life standards. Include worship, skits, games, songs, food. Involve everyone in planning and some kind of responsibility for the celebration, perhaps by dividing into committees.

Alternative Celebrations Catalogue, from Alternatives; see below.

Another Kind of Christmas, $2.00 by Meredith Sommers Dregni, Hunger Action Coalition, 122 W. Franklin, Minneapolis, MN 55404 (A three-session curriculum on traditions and giving, for families and groups.)

15 min.

Filmstrip, "The Celebration Revolution of Alexander Scrooge," from Alternatives, P.O. Box 1707, Forest Park, GA 30050. A cartoon story about gift giving.

30 min.

Making a pledge. A commitment to living more with less. Two suggestions:
1. Hand out the Shakertown Pledge and have individuals or families read it and make a commitment to a specific action. Write it on paper and read at closing worship.
2. Repeat charades, but have it be an action their family is going to do and apply life standards which fit.

Shakertown Pledge*

WHAT WOULD YOU DO IF...?
A role playing exercise.

Purpose
To help participants handle situations of nonconformity.

Time
About 20 minutes.

Plan
To role play or talk about situations in pairs, using the suggested situations or those of the group. This can also be done in front of a large group by asking for volunteers to role play.

Setting
Area where pairs of participants can talk to each other.

Process
Write the following situations on a board or duplicate them for each pair, or create situations of nonconformity with the group. Divide into pairs. Have one participant read or act out this situation, the other respond to it.

What would you do if . . .
   —a vegetarian came to dinner at your house?
   —your friend threw away his/her television set?
   —your neighbor asked to take the bus downtown together even
      though you had offered to drive your car?
   —you saw someone collecting cans and bottles and trash along the
      road?
   —your neighbors built wind and solar collectors for energy in their
      home?
   —your sister or brother dated someone of a different race?
   —you were on a team which never won any games?
   —your friend quit a job which involved making weapons for the
      army?
   —you were given a membership in Bread for the World in place of a
      "real" gift?
   —your friends wanted you to buy expensive shoes, even though
      the shoes didn't fit into your budget?

As a wrap-up read the story of the Good Samaritan or tell it in your own words (Lk. 10:20-37). Instead of finishing the story, let the participants add their ending. Or dramatize the story. Help them understand how the Samaritan was not conforming to standards in his country.

THE GOOD LIFE
An exercise on pressures to consume and conform.

Purpose

To illustrate pressures on us to conform to the "goods" life in America rather than the "good" life in Christ.

Plan

To make two collages—one which shows the "goods" life as promoted by our culture, the other to show the "good" life in Christ. Follow this with a discussion.

Supplies

Materials to make collages: variety of magazines, scissors, tape or paste, newsprint, markers, Bibles.

Time

15 minutes in small groups, 15-minute discussion in large group.

Process

Divide into small groups from four to five persons each, with table or floor space. Hand out supplies, including two pieces of newsprint, to each small group. Tell them to make two collages, cutting up magazines, drawing pictures, or writing words or phrases. Title one collage "The Goods Life," the other "The Good Life."

When collages are finished, bring the groups together. Hang up the collages and ask the small groups to talk about them. When this is finished, use the following questions, or your own:

What are the differences or similarities between the two collages? How do you feel when you see the collages next to each other?

What do you do to lessen the impact of advertisements which tell you that you are not okay without their products?

Complete this sentence, then talk about it: "One way in which I am a nonconformist is—"

Who are people who support and encourage you to think and act in ways which are congruent with your beliefs? Whom do you support?

KEEPING SCORE
By Ann Herbert

In the beginning, God didn't make just two people; he made a bunch of people. Because he wanted us to have a lot of fun, and he said you can't really have fun unless there's a whole gang of you. He put us in Eden which was a combination garden and playground and park and told us to have fun.

At first we did have fun just like he expected. We rolled down the hills, waded in the streams, climbed on the trees, swung on the vines, ran in the meadows, frolicked in the woods, hid in the forest, and acted silly. We laughed a lot.

Then one day this snake told us that we weren't having real fun because we weren't keeping score. Back then, we didn't know what score was. When he explained it, we still couldn't see the fun. But he said we should give an apple to the person who was best at all the games and we'd never know who was best without keeping score. We could see the fun of that, of course, because we were all sure we were best.

It was different after that. We yelled a lot. We had to make up new scoring rules for most of the games. Others—such as frolicking—we stopped playing because they were too hard to score.

By the time God found out what had happened we were spending about 45 minutes a day actually playing and the rest of the time working out scoring. God was wroth about that—very, very wroth. He said we couldn't use his garden anymore because we weren't having fun. We told him we were having lots of fun. He was just being narrowminded because it wasn't exactly the kind of fun he originally thought of.

He wouldn't listen.

He kicked us out, and he said we couldn't come back until we stopped keeping score. To rub it in (to get our attention, he said), he told us we were all going to die and our scores wouldn't mean anything anyway.

He was wrong. My cumulative, all-game score now is 16,548 and that means a lot to me. If I can raise it to 20,000 before I die, I'll know I've accomplished something. Even if I can't, my life has a great deal of meaning because I've taught my children to score high and they'll be able to reach 20,000 or even 30,000.

Really, it was life in the garden that didn't mean anything. Fun is great in its place but without scoring there's no reason for it. God actually has a very superficial view of life and I'm certainly glad my children are being raised away from his influence. We were lucky. We're all very grateful to the snake.

THE SHAKERTOWN PLEDGE

Recognizing that the earth and the fullness thereof is a gift from our gracious God, and that we are called to cherish, nurture, and provide loving stewardship for the earth's resources,

And recognizing that life itself is a gift, and a call to responsibility, joy, and celebration,

I make the following declarations:

1. I declare myself to be a world citizen.

2. I commit myself to lead an ecologically sound life.

3. I commit myself to lead a life of creative simplicity and to share my personal wealth with the world's poor.

4. I commit myself to join with others in reshaping institutions in order to bring about a more just global society in which each person has full access to the needed resources for their physical, emotional, intellectual, and spiritual growth.

5. I commit myself to occupational accountability, and in so doing I will seek to avoid the creation of products which cause harm to others.

6. I affirm the gift of my body, and commit myself to its proper nourishment and physical well-being.

7. I commit myself to examine continually my relations with others, and to attempt to relate honestly, morally, and lovingly to those around me.

8. I commit myself to personal renewal through prayer, meditation, and study.

9. I commit myself to responsible participation in a community of faith.

MEDITATION BASED ON THE BEATITUDES

People who do not hold tightly to things are happy,
    because all of God's kingdom is theirs.
People who are gentle with the earth will see it blossom forever.
People who can cry for all the world's suffering,
    will live to see happiness.
People who hunger and thirst for what is right,
    will finally have their fill.
People who really care,
    will find love wherever they go.
People who don't let the world get them down,
    will see God.
People who make peace happen,
    are God's children.
People who give up their own comfort so that others can be helped,
    know what heaven is all about.
LORD, LET US BE LIKE THESE!

—From THE EMPTY PLACE, copyright 1976 by Franciscan Communications Center. Used by permission.

SIMPLE GIFTS

'Tis the gift to be simple, 'tis a gift to be free,
'Tis a gift to come down where we ought to be,
And when we find ourselves in the place just right
'Twill be in the valley of love and delight.

When true simplicity is gained
To bow and to bend we shall not be ashamed
To turn, turn 'twill be our delight
'Till in turning, turning we come 'round right.

AGENCIES INVOLVED IN RELIEF/DEVELOPMENT PROGRAMS/JUSTICE EDUCATION

ALC Hunger Program
422 S. 5th Street
Minneapolis, MN 55415

Alternatives
P. O. Box 1707
Forest Park, GA 30051

American Baptist Churches
World Relief Committee
P. O. Box 851
Valley Forge, PA 19482-0851

American Friends Service Committee
  (AFSC)
1501 Cherry Street
Philadelphia, PA 19102

Catholic Relief Services (CRS)
350 Fifth Avenue
New York, NY 10001

Christian Reformed World Relief
  Committee
2850 Kalamazoo S.E.
Grand Rapids, MI 49560

Church World Service
Office on Global Education
2115 North Charles Street
Baltimore, MD 21218

Episcopal Hunger Program
815 Second Avenue
New York, NY 10017

LCA World Hunger Appeal
231 Madison Avenue
New York, NY 10016

Lutheran World Relief (LWR)
360 Park Avenue South
New York, NY 10010

Mennonite Central Committee (MCC)
Box M
Akron, PA 17501

MCC (Canada)
201-1483 Pembina Highway
Winnipeg, Manitoba R3T 2C8

Oxfam America
302 Columbus Avenue
Boston, MA 02116

Oxfam of Canada
251 Lauier Avenue, West
Ottawa, Ontario K1P 5J9

Presbyterian Hunger Program
475 Riverside Drive
Room 1268
New York, NY 10115
  or
341 Ponce de Leon Ave. NE
Atlanta, GA 30365

UCC Office of Hunger Action
  Coordination
475 Riverside Dr., 16th Floor
New York, NY 10115

UMC Board of Discipleship
Hunger Program
P. O. Box 840
Nashville, TN 37202

United Methodist Committee on
  Relief
475 Riverside Dr.
Room 1374
New York, NY 10115

World Neighbors
5116 N. Portland Ave.
Oklahoma City, OK 73112

World Relief
P. O. Box WRC
Wheaton, IL 60189

World Vision International
Box O
Pasadena, CA 91109

THE AUTHOR

Pines outline the edge of a large grassy field enclosing twenty-three tents. It is a warm Independence Holiday weekend and the camp residents are with the author as facilitator while experiencing and sharing "more with less." The curriculum, a practical companion piece to the book, *Living More with Less* by Doris Longacre, was developed from a need perceived by Meredith Sommers Dregni.

A person with a global perspective and sensitivity to issues of justice, Meredith's writings provide encouragement toward congruence, simplicity, and depth in lifestyle. Her work parallels her own journey toward truths and realities amidst an often discordant world. A unique attentiveness to her own internal intuitive concerns is reflected in the curriculum and guides users toward a shared future with hope for all. The author hopes that the curriculum can bring these ideas into sharp focus for each of us in the process of experiencing "more with less."

Meredith is a Minnesotan by birth and a world citizen in thought. She has lived in Virginia, rural Michigan and Minnesota, plus London and Brussels, but always returns to Minnesota. She is married and mother of three sons. A humanities honors graduate of the University of Minnesota, she dedicates considerable effort to reading and studying world hunger, lifestyle change, and related issues.

Meredith is a complex, perceptive, and discriminating person.

These traits serve her well in writing. Although she is dedicated to change, she admits that change to a different lifestyle is occasionally frightening and lonely. She has also described it as both inclusive and exclusive depending upon supportive colleagues and one's place in society. She is co-founder of the Hunger Action Coalition, the Twin City-based organization dedicated to solving the problem of hunger in the world by attacking root causes. Active nationally, Meredith serves on the committee of the Presbyterian Hunger Program. Recently she traveled with a national church group to Nicaragua and Costa Rica to obtain direct knowledge about political, economic, and social issues in these countries. Her writings include magazine articles and a curriculum piece entitled *Another Kind of Christmas.*

Meredith is a warm person, exciting to know and love. (Written by her husband, Jay Dregni, February 6, 1983)